For Vivienne, Julian and Ryder, who will heal the world.
And for Barbara, who guided me to do my part –A.K.

For Ricardo, who always believed I could fill the world with drawings.
And for Mum and Dad, who I thank for everything –M.R.

Earth's Aquarium

Discover 15 Real-Life Water Worlds

written by
ALEXANDER KAUFMAN

illustrated by
MARIANA RODRIGUES

MAGIC CAT PUBLISHING

NEW YORK

FOREWORD

For as long as I can remember I have been obsessed by wild water and all the fantastic creatures that live in, on, and all around it. I caught my first fish at four, tended my own frog pond at six, and met my first seal before I could ride a bike. I can't even begin to imagine what my life would be like without all that time spent staring at water, pondering the answers to the most important question:

What lives down there?

I have been incredibly fortunate to live waterside throughout my life, at a time when the wonders of that magical watery curtain remain out of reach for so many. Water worlds don't actually give up their secrets all that easily. It takes time, timing, and often a healthy dose of imagination, before that seemingly blank void starts to reveal its magnificent truths. Luckily, this book gives any reader a place to start connecting with our water worlds, right at a time when a heightened interest in the aquatic environment could not be more vital.

Sadly, our aquatic environments are facing threats today like never before. Climate change, pollution, human-made barriers, over-abstraction and severe overexploitation have all helped drive many of our waterways and their inhabitants to the very brink of extinction. Really though, how can you expect people to care about something they seldom even notice?

Earth's Aquarium helps bridge the gap in our knowledge and brings an all-new passion for water in all its forms. This beautifully illustrated book introduces us to stunning coral reefs, Amazonian riverscapes, kelp forests, and a multitude of less-than-classical environments like mudflats, estuaries, wetlands, and the mangroves. Many of these important locations prop up ecosystems that should naturally be teeming with wildlife.

Use this book to spend more time looking for the magic element in water, and become a champion for change before time runs out.

—Will Millard

fisherman, explorer, and broadcaster

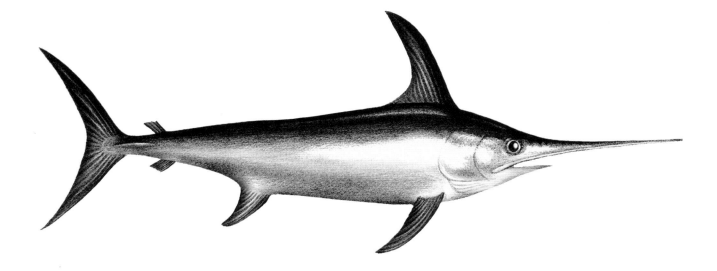

CONTENTS

WATER IS LIFE

Water is life. The slogan grew popular over recent years as activists fought to prevent pollution of freshwater sources from which humans derive drinking water. Our towns and cities and nations are overwhelmingly located near water–to transport our goods and people, energize our homes and factories, and quench our crops and thirst. Our songs and poems and paintings often feature water. Our bodies are mostly made up of water.

Water also contains life. Lots of it. Scientists have cataloged more than 235,725 individual marine species. But the total is estimated to be millions upon millions more. The oceans cover the vast majority of our planet. Rivers and streams vein the continents where we live. Ancient lakes and ponds pockmark our landscapes, filled by frozen behemoths from a distant age. Within these bodies of water are creatures so diverse and vibrant language fails to capture their range. Giant whales. Microscopic bacteria. Verdant grass. Electric fish.

The stunning distinctions in organisms demonstrates the complex chemistry that defines ecosystems as vast as an ocean and as modest as a puddle. The combination of stinging salt, crushing pressure, and cocktails of prehistoric water sources give way to such a variety of life that it should give any person pause. Far from looking to the cosmos for a sense of wonder and smallness, one must only look to the marsh, the lake, or the sea to feel humbled.

And yet, the impact we are having on these systems far exceeds even our wildest expectations. More than a century of modern pollution is dramatically changing these ecosystems, threatening to unravel a web of life spun over millions of years of evolution. To save it will require changing our ways. But to do so, we must first understand and learn to love that which is so close to us, and yet so alien. May that journey begin here.

Salinity

Salt originates as a mineral in rock. But the compound is found virtually everywhere, from all the water on Earth to the blood in our bodies. The concentration of salt, known as salinity, defines the three major categories of water. If you think of water as a crowd of particles, imagine dissolved salt as people in that crowd wearing blue shirts. Salt water contains average salinity levels of 35 parts per thousand, meaning about 35 of 1,000 people are wearing blue shirts. By contrast, fresh water–the stuff we drink–averages salt levels of 0.5 parts per thousand, or just half a blue shirt. Brackish water, the category in between, falls anywhere between 0.5 and 30 parts per thousand.

Salt water is, by far, the most abundant type of water on our planet. The oceans cover 70 percent of the Earth's surface. As such, salt water makes up 97 percent of all water. Fresh water comprises just 2.5 percent of all water. Of that, 69 percent is frozen in glaciers and ice caps, 30 percent is found underground, and just over 1 percent is located on the surface of lakes, ponds, and rivers. Brackish water, typically formed in estuaries, marshes and other places where fresh water and salt water meet, comprises less than 1 percent of all water on the planet.

All life on this planet began in the oceans, so salt is a necessary component to all creatures. But life evolved as more fish, plants, and reptiles took advantage of freshwater ecosystems. And as those adapted to new environments, their tolerance to salt changed and their bodies morphed to either expel or hold onto salt in the water. The kidneys of freshwater fish often function to push out excess water while maintaining salinity levels. Saltwater fish, by contrast, have special enzymes in the gills to get rid of salt when salinity levels get too high.

Too much salt can be deadly. There is one giant lake bordered by Israel, Jordan, and the Palestinian West Bank, where salinity concentrations are a thirst-inducing 280 parts per thousand. Its name? The Dead Sea.

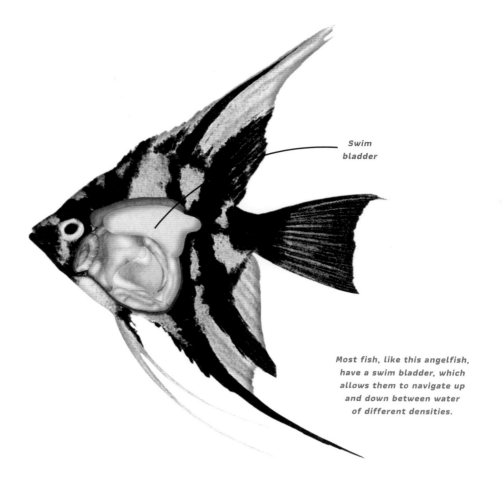

Swim bladder

Most fish, like this angelfish, have a swim bladder, which allows them to navigate up and down between water of different densities.

Density

The density of water describes how closely the people wearing shirts in the crowd are packed together. Salinity and temperature affect density. The warmer and less salty the water, the less dense it is. The colder and saltier the water, the denser it is. So tropical fresh water is the least dense. Cold salt water, like that in the Southern Ocean, is the densest.

That temperature dynamic, however, is only true when water is in its liquid form. Have you ever noticed that ice cubes float? That's because water expands when it freezes, meaning water at 39° Fahrenheit, or 4° Celsius, is more dense than water at 32° Fahrenheit, or 0° Celsius. This phenomenon is vital to life in lakes and ponds, for example. In winter, when some water freezes, it stays near the surface, forming a protective layer that insulates the warmer water below, where fish, turtles, plants, and other marine life wait out the cold until spring.

The density of water is constantly changing. But global warming is having a major effect on density, which is changing the oceans. Ice in the Arctic is melting extremely fast, adding more fresh water to oceans. That fresh water decreases the density of the salt water, causing sea levels to rise. It's also altering currents, weakening the balance between cold water and warm water currents and rapidly increasing the temperature of certain bodies of water.

The changes can take a toll on marine life. Most fish, for example, have swim bladders that help them adjust their buoyancy to differences in water density. But changes to salinity, which in turn affects density, can alter the buoyancy of fish eggs and larvae, making it harder for some baby fish to survive.

Salmon spend the first months of their lives in fresh water, then swim downstream into the salt water of the ocean, before returning upstream again when they are ready to spawn in fresh water.

Light penetration

Humans and sunlight have something in common: They can't travel that deep into water.

The upper layer of the ocean, from the surface down to about 650 feet, is known as the euphotic zone—"photic" coming from the word *photon*, or particle of light. In this sunlit zone, the sun is bright and plentiful enough for photosynthesis to occur. Most ocean fish live here, as do coral, sea turtles, and zooplankton.

From a depth of 650 feet to 3,000 feet, things start to get dark and murky. This is called the disphotic zone. In this twilight zone, there is light, but not enough for plants to generate food. But the fish, sea stars, and urchins that call this zone home feed on bits of algae and plant matter that fall from the upper sunlit zone, while whales in turn feed on them. Many animals adapted to this layer of the ocean have large eyes to capture any traces of light— and large teeth to snag prey.

Below 3,000 feet is the aphotic zone. This midnight zone is bathed in inky blackness. No light can penetrate here.

Yet lightlessness does not equate to lifelessness. Deep in the darkness, some marine creatures develop bioluminescence. These organisms' bodies contain a chemical called luciferin that, when it mixes with oxygen, produces light. Bioluminescent jellyfish, algae, and fish will light up when it's time to mate or feed. Because plants cannot grow in the darkness, fauna in the aphotic zone tend to be carnivores. But that isn't the only source of food. Deep-sea vents spew chemicals and minerals that feed bacteria and worms. Other creatures are expert scavengers, gathering scraps that float down from better-lit zones or filtering particles of organic matter from the water.

Cuvier's beaked whale dives close to 10,000 feet, where it experiences pressure 100 times of that at the surface. It has adapted to have a rib cage that can fold down to stop the air from completely compressing in its lungs.

Currents

Waves aren't the only movement in the water. Currents serve as fast roads, carrying water, animals, and nutrients thousands of miles down rivers and around oceans.

Rivers gush water from a source—often an underground spring or a frozen glacier—that is then carried by gravity to the ocean. The ocean's currents are even more complex. Differences in density, salinity, and temperature cause fast-moving channels of water to form. These currents serve as the arteries of the ocean, circulating water throughout the system.

Take, for example, the Labrador Current. This current is formed by cold water melting off Greenland. Due to its temperature, the water is pushed downward and pulsed southward down North America's eastern coast. The Gulf of Mexico, meanwhile, pushes warm water northward through the mighty Gulf Stream. The interaction of the two currents is often called the heartbeat of the Atlantic Ocean.

Yet climate change is causing a heart murmur. The increased volume of cold water melting from Greenland's ice sheet is changing the density and salinity of the water, and weakening the Labrador Current. The increased heat of the Gulf Stream is lowering the density and causing the current to weaken. The combined effect slows the circulation of the ocean, heightening sea levels and causing potentially catastrophic effects on ecosystems that developed over millions of years under certain conditions, with whales, sharks, and sea turtles, among others, relying on ocean currents to locate annual breeding and feeding grounds.

Pressure

We're under pressure all the time. When we're standing at sea level, the air around us presses down on us at a measurement of one atmosphere, while the fluids in our bodies push back with roughly the same force, creating an equilibrium.

Things change once we dive into the ocean. Liquid exerts what's called hydrostatic pressure on objects. The deeper we go, the more that force increases. That's why we feel the pressure change in our eardrums as we submerge further. It's pressure.

Pressure increases by one atmosphere roughly every 30 feet we go down. Humans aren't used to navigating sharp changes in pressure. Divers who go too deep then come up too fast can suffer decompression sickness, sometimes called the bends, when nitrogen in the body forms bubbles as a result of the pressure change and causes severe pain in the joints and bones. Any scuba dive below 130 feet is considered ultra-deep diving, while the world record for the deepest dive by a human ever was just over 1,000 feet. But other animals are specially adapted to cruise between pressure levels.

Whales, for example, can collapse their lungs when diving deep down. Fish who dwell deep under the water, at pressures that would crush a human body, contain small, organic molecules called piezolytes. These recently discovered molecules prevent pressure from crushing membranes, protein, and other parts of a fish's body. Piezolytes are also what give sea creatures their fishy smell.

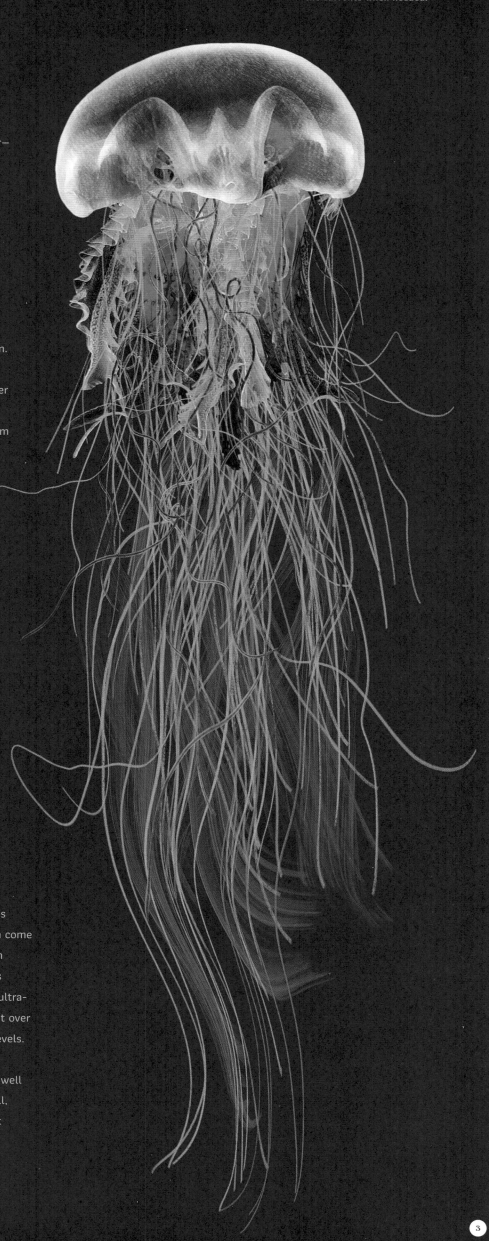

Waves

Ponds can be placid. But the oceans, seas, and big lakes are never still. Waves are constant. In extreme events, like an earthquake or underwater volcanic eruption, giant waves called tsunamis can form as the shockwaves and force displace massive amounts of water. But most waves are whipped up by wind, caused by the friction between the surface of the water and the gusts of air. Others are caused by the gravitational pull of the sun and moon, which creates tides.

Coastal ecosystems are shaped by waves. Creatures that live in tidal pools are adapted to withstand the force of lapping waves. Limpets have strong feet that help them clutch the substrate. Mussels and barnacles excrete adhesives that cling them to rocks, even when battered by rough waves.

But the decades to come may test the integrity of even the strongest tidal ecosystems. Research shows that climate change is making waves bigger and more powerful. Left unchecked, scientists project the changes caused by global temperature increases from human pollution will significantly alter the waves in 50 percent of the Earth's coastal habitats.

Waves could help fight climate change, too. Coal, oil, and natural gas burned to create electricity is one of the world's largest sources of climate change pollution. While many countries and companies are starting to build solar panels and windmills to capture energy from the sun and wind, some are experimenting with generating power from the waves. Europeans have generated energy at mills using tidal energy for centuries, but now there are power plants that convert the energy of waves into electricity in China, France, Russia, and South Korea.

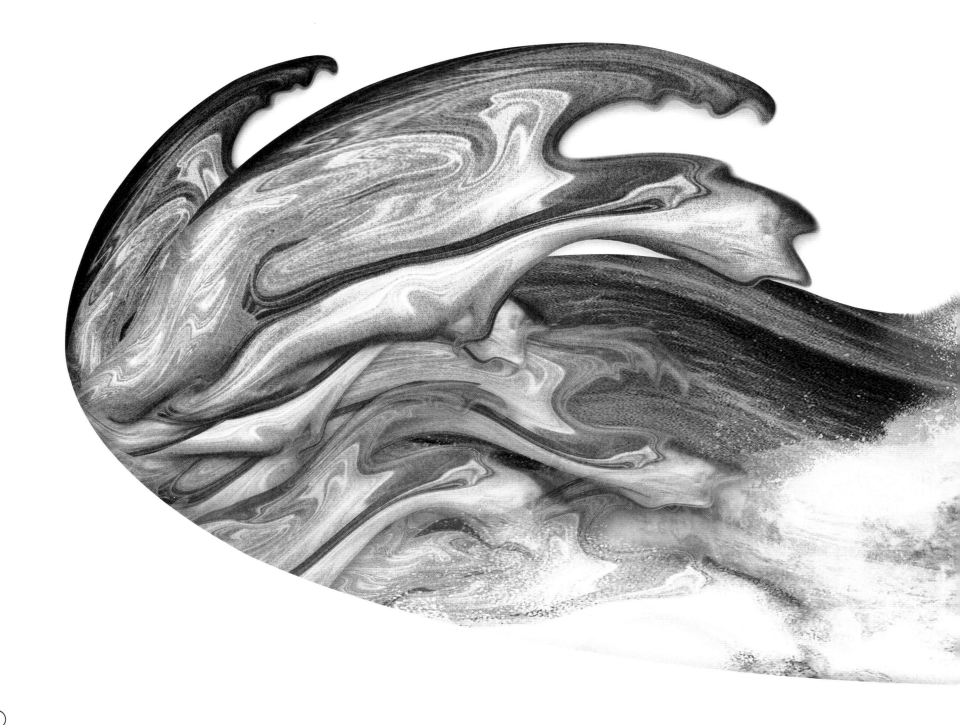

Water acidity

In the 1700s, humans in Europe and North America started burning tremendous amounts of coal to generate electricity and power factories. By the 1900s, that trend expanded to include oil and gas. These fossil fuels powered many advancements in human society. But they also filled the atmosphere with carbon dioxide. This pollution creates a blanket around the Earth, trapping heat from the sun and raising the planet's temperature. Since the start of the industrial age, concentrations of carbon dioxide in the atmosphere have soared from 280 parts per million to well over 400 parts per million. Humans have never in our history existed on a planet with so much carbon dioxide in the air.

The problem doesn't just stay above us. The oceans sop up about one third of all human-caused carbon dioxide pollution. Once absorbed, the carbon dioxide changes the pH of the ocean, making the water more acidic. The oceans today are at least 25 percent more acidic than they were before the industrial era.

At first, scientists didn't worry about ocean acidification. They figured that rivers would carry chemicals and minerals from rocks into the ocean and balance out the changes. But the enormous amount of carbon dioxide humans emitted—and are still producing more of every year—overwhelmed that natural system.

This is one of the biggest crises ever faced by life in the oceans. Higher acidity levels are killing off plankton, shellfish, and corals, whose reefs die off and turn white in events called bleaching. Whales and fish suffer as the food chain is disrupted. Scientists studying ancient rocks found that similar acidity levels existed more than 250 million years ago . . . and triggered an event called the Great Dying, where 90 percent of all marine species went extinct.

Tides & oxygen concentration

Throughout the day, the moon's gravity causes the Earth's water to swell on the sides of the planet closest and furthest away. This effect causes high tides and low tides. This giant, macro phenomenon causes dramatic and important changes in relatively tiny ecosystems.

Consider life in marshes of small tidal flats where water pools on coastal shores when the tide goes out. For half the day, these shallow pools roast under the sun, and the snails, shrimp, and small fish that wind up in them must survive predators on the hunt and increasingly warm waters. They must also endure lower oxygen levels. The life in these pools absorb much of the limited supply of oxygen in the water.

That all changes once the tide comes rushing back. Fresh seawater flushes into the pools, replenishing the supply of oxygen-rich water.

This stands in contrast to how oxygen returns to stiller bodies of water, such as swamps and ponds. There, algae and plant life grows and is able to take root without fear of briny waves washing in and ripping out young plants by the roots. That flora produces oxygen that enriches the water for gill-breathing creatures like fish.

But both oxygenation processes face a grave threat from global warming. In freshwater lagoons and ponds, increased temperatures can deplete oxygen, as can algae that is not getting enough sunlight. In the oceans, weakened currents are decreasing circulation and deoxygenating the water. Over the past 50 years, oxygen levels in the oceans have depleted by 2 percent on average.

Limpets have multilayered outer shells to withstand the impact of waves.

MUDFLATS

It's a cool, crisp morning. You step off the sandy beach and squish your feet into the soft, brown mud. The tide is out, and a muddy landscape of exposed seafloor stretches out before you as far as the eye can see.

This is the Wadden Sea, the world's largest unbroken intertidal system of sand, wetlands, and mudflats. Spanning more than 5,500 square miles from the northern coast of the Netherlands and Germany to Denmark's southwestern shore, the Wadden traces its history back more than 8,000 years, when the melting of glaciers that once covered much of the Earth slowed down.

The Earth may have stopped changing dramatically enough for the sea to form, but dramatic changes define the Wadden, and make it home

to some of the richest biodiversity in this part of the world.

While the outer zone of the sea remains permanently underwater, the middle zone that encompasses roughly 40 percent of the area drains every 12 hours when the tide recedes. What remains is a banquet feast of worms and shellfish for the birds that make the Wadden their home.

Look up, and you'll see all kinds of birds soaring overhead. On the ground, you see a gull that looks like it's dancing in the mud. But that's no jig it's doing with its feet. The gull is actually kneading the mud to soften it and push little cockles up to the surface. The early bird gets the bivalve.

The trouble here is that the Earth is once again changing, and this time because of humans. Fumes from burning oil and gas are heating the planet and causing the glaciers on the planet's poles to melt, and seas to rise. In the next century, that percentage of mudflat that's exposed every day is going to get smaller and smaller until there will be very little left.

And it's not just that the seas are swelling again. Companies drill for gas under the Wadden itself. When the drilling is done, and the gas is sucked out from far underground, the seafloor will sink lower and lower. Now scientists are worried about the future of the creatures who live here.

1. Nilsson's pipefish
Syngnathus rostellatus

Nilsson's pipefish may look like a worm, but this skinny fish is a specially adapted survivor. Male pipefish incubate eggs until they're hatched into fully formed babies, essentially giving birth to them then directing the babies' narrow, armored mouths to feed on the larvae of shellfish on the mudflat.

2. Asian shore crab
Hemigrapsus takanoi

The Asian shore crab is not native to these waters. These hardy crustaceans, known also as the brush-clawed shore crab, first appeared in the Wadden in the early 2000s after attaching to boats in ports in Japan and China and traveling all the way to Europe. As so-called opportunistic omnivores, these crabs will eat just about any food they can fit in their mouths.

3. Pied avocet
Recurvirostra avosetta

The pied avocet is among the dozens of species of migratory birds that make stops at the Wadden to breed, lay eggs, and grab a meal. Its long, spindly legs allow it to wade into shallow water to hunt without taking a swim.

4. Harbor seal
Phoca vitulina

Both the harbor seal and its bigger cousin, the grey seal, make use of the sandbanks that dot the outer portions of the sea to breed, rest, and shed their furry coats in a process known as molting. Humans almost wiped out these species, but a ban on hunting them has helped them recover.

Species that live in
MUDFLATS

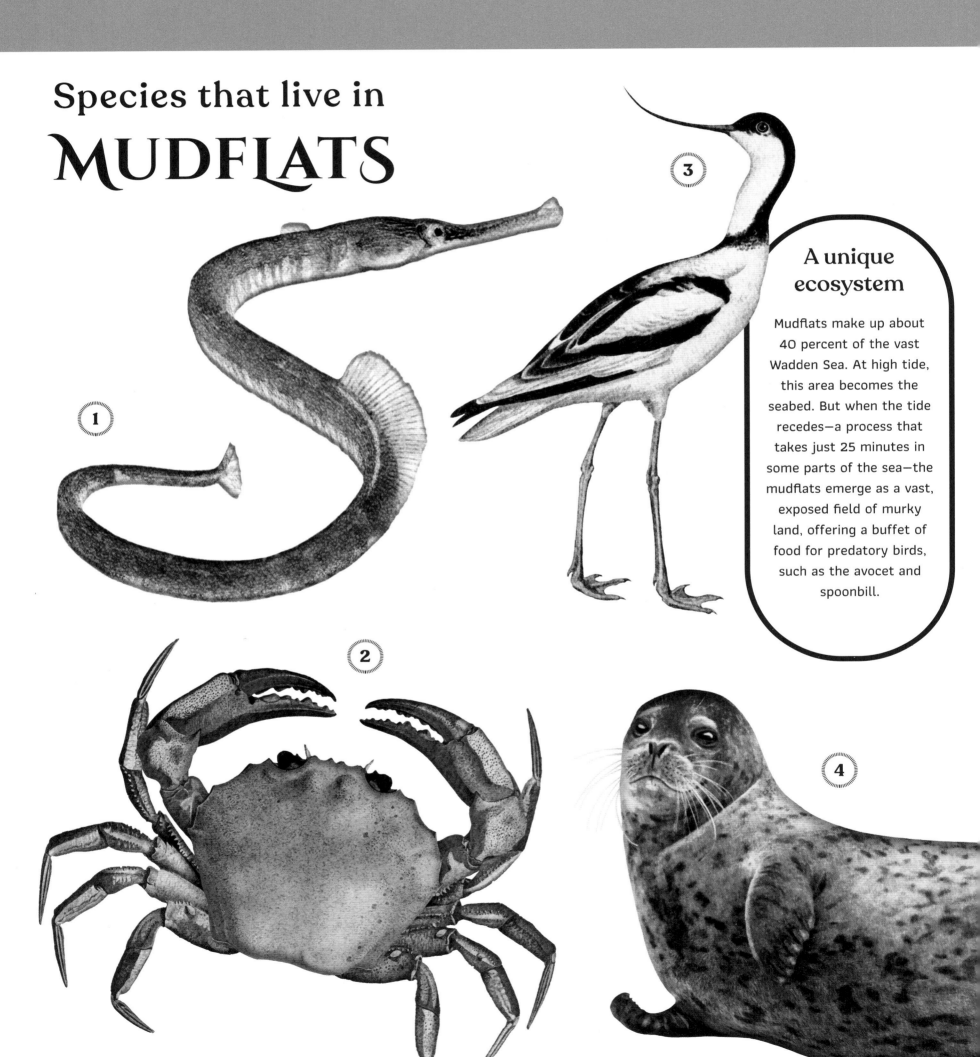

A unique ecosystem

Mudflats make up about 40 percent of the vast Wadden Sea. At high tide, this area becomes the seabed. But when the tide recedes—a process that takes just 25 minutes in some parts of the sea—the mudflats emerge as a vast, exposed field of murky land, offering a buffet of food for predatory birds, such as the avocet and spoonbill.

5. Eurasian spoonbill
Platalea leucorodia

Dozens of species of migratory birds, including the spoonbill, avocet, and gull-billed tern, make stops at the Wadden to breed, lay eggs, and grab a meal. Some gulls are known to knead their feet to loosen the mud and drive their shellfish prey to the surface.

6. Mudsnail
Hydrobia ulvae

The scientific name of the mudsnail, or Laver spire shell, points toward where it likes to hide: within *Ulva lactuca*, or sea lettuce. But what really distinguishes these snails is their ability to float through the water aboard a raft of mucus.

7. Bullrout
Myoxocephalus scorpius

From above, it's hard to see the bullrout. These tough roundfish are demersal, meaning they live close to the seafloor. They camouflage into the muddy, rocky ground with splotchy brown coloring. It's the perfect disguise to hunt in. These fish are ambush predators who feed on other fish and crustaceans.

8. European flounder
Platichthys flesus

The flounder can endure salt water, fresh water, and brackish conditions. But this flat-bodied bottom feeder prefers to lay its eggs in the shallow coastal salt water, where there is more oxygen than in freshwater estuaries but fewer of the predators found in deeper water.

9. Lugworm
Arenicola marina

When the water retreats, the mudflat is covered with tiny mounds that look, well, a little like . . . dog poo. These structures, sometimes called "spaghetti hills," are actually casts of sand left behind when lugworms, or sandworms, burrow into the sand. Typically out of sight unless a bird or a fisherman looking for bait catches one, these mounds make visible what's beneath the seafloor.

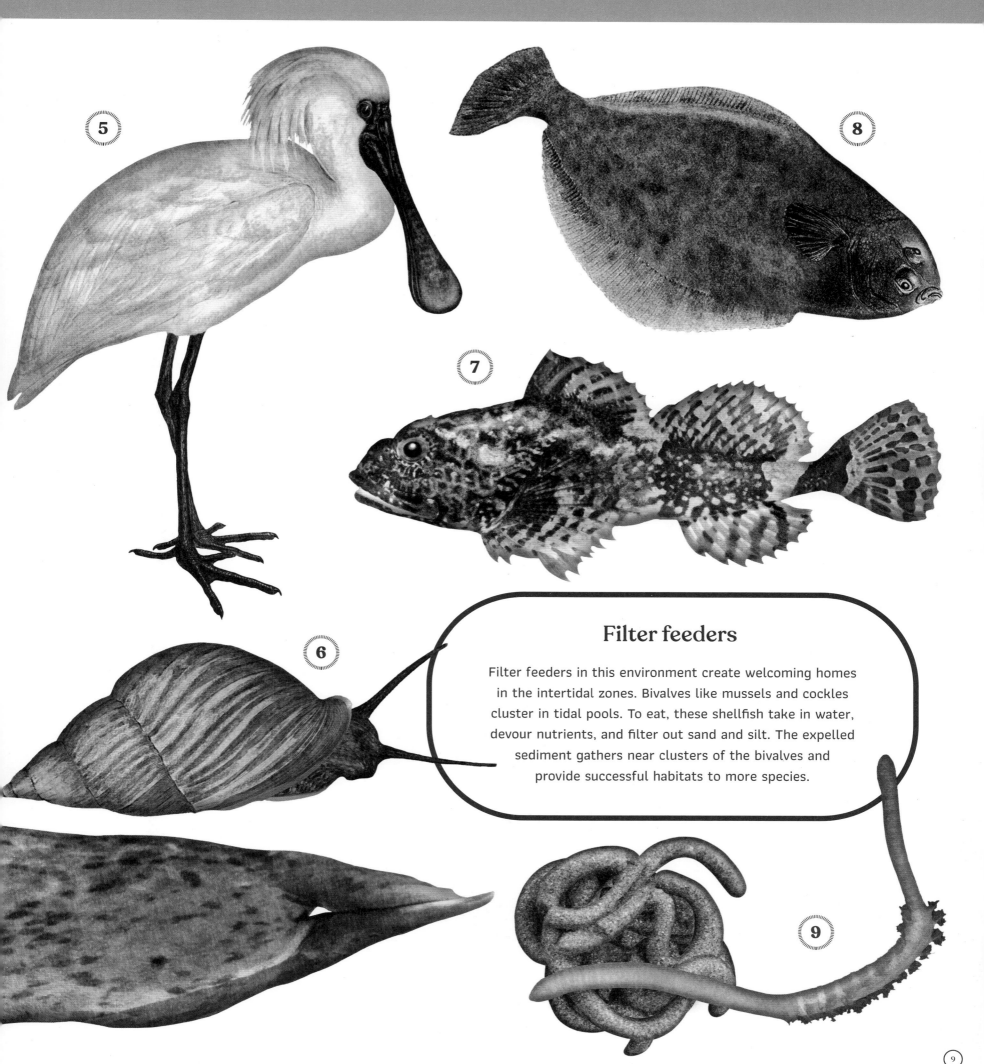

Filter feeders

Filter feeders in this environment create welcoming homes in the intertidal zones. Bivalves like mussels and cockles cluster in tidal pools. To eat, these shellfish take in water, devour nutrients, and filter out sand and silt. The expelled sediment gathers near clusters of the bivalves and provide successful habitats to more species.

MANGROVE FOREST

By the time you paddle your kayak up to the edge of the Phang Nga mangrove forest, you're getting really sweaty in the humid heat of tropical Southeast Asia. But what you see before you is a distraction from the soaked T-shirt clinging to your chest.

There's plenty to take in. Limestone cliffs surround and jut out of blue-green estuaries that flow into the Phang Nga Bay, a large basin near the Straits of Malacca. Among the dense green foliage overhead, birds, reptiles, and insects skitter from branch to seamless branch. But trace those branches down, and you see something

astonishing: The trees themselves appear to be weaving a giant basket.

This is what makes mangroves so special. The brambled roots of these trees grow submerged in the murky, blue-green water that leads out to Phang Nga Bay. These roots both hold the ecosystem together and create a city of aquatic life beneath the surface of the water.

But even this protected area of Thailand is at risk. Humans cut down mangrove trees to carve and burn as wood. A growing human population's increasing appetite for seafood has prompted some farmers here to cut down mangroves to make room for shrimp farms.

Yet the biggest threat to these forests is sea level rising from a warming climate. While mangrove roots are meant to stay underwater, the trees will die if water levels rise too high, and the new influx of salt water completely alters the balance of the natural brackish mixture found here, making it harder for this species—and all the others that have evolved to live in this unique habitat—to survive.

1. Mangrove jack
Lutjanus argentimaculatus

The mangrove jack is a powerful and clever carnivore. This fish, sometimes known as a sea perch, hides among the rocky bottom near the roots of mangrove trees, watching for prey. When it locates a target, it explodes out in a fury, catching its prey by surprise.

2. Chinese pond heron
Ardeola bacchus

The Chinese pond heron is distinguished by its red head and neck, blue back, and white breast. One of six species of pond heron, it is known to get along with its cousins. These birds will often raise their young with other species in nesting colonies known as heronries.

3. Sea snail
Laevistrombus canarium

This sea snail, also known as the dog conch, is found commonly across Thailand and Southeast Asia. It grazes on the seabed, and will even devour sand in order to suck the algae and bacterial film off the grains.

4. Mangrove snake
Boiga dendrophila

By day, you might mistake the mangrove snake, also known as the gold-ringed cat snake, for a dark vine hanging from the trees. By night, it descends to feed on rodents, frogs, fish, and insects that crawl among the mangrove roots. Growing up to 8 feet long, these are among the largest cat snakes in the world, and they're strong swimmers, too.

5. Bobtail squid
Idiosepius thailandicus

At only a few millimeters long, the bobtail squid is considered one of the smallest known cephalopods in the world. Females' mantles, portions of squids that aren't tentacles, grow no longer than 10 millimeters, while males' are 7 millimeters at full length. To stay safe from predators, these tiny spotted creatures lay their eggs in the roots of the mangroves.

Species that live in the
MANGROVE FOREST

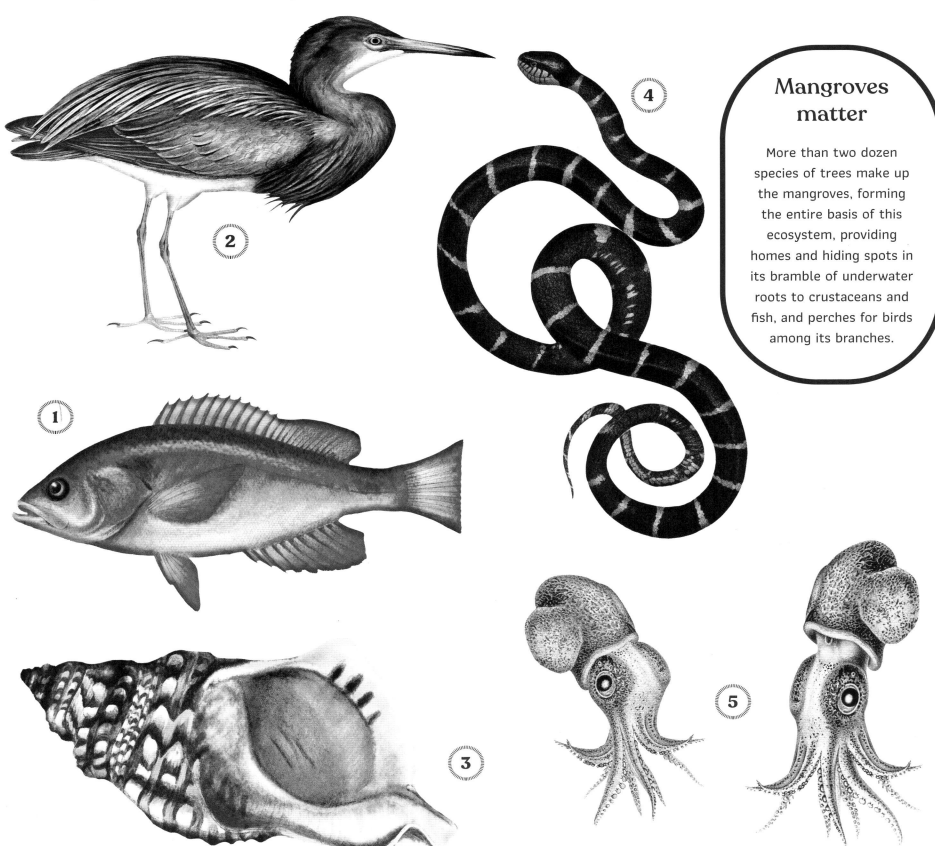

Mangroves matter

More than two dozen species of trees make up the mangroves, forming the entire basis of this ecosystem, providing homes and hiding spots in its bramble of underwater roots to crustaceans and fish, and perches for birds among its branches.

6. Northern river terrapin
Batagur baska

The northern river terrapin is a slick turtle with an angular shell, a rounded brown head, and a pinkish-orange neck. It is hunted for meat by humans and is considered critically endangered.

7. Brown-winged kingfisher
Pelargopsis amauroptera

The brown-winged kingfisher is an extraordinary bird with chocolate-colored wings, a blue tail, and a yellow head. But it's the sharp, bright orange bullet-shaped beak that stands out—and makes the kingfisher a formidable predator, able to chomp down fish and crabs.

8. Soldier crab
Mictyris thailandensis

Species of soldier crabs exist across Southeast Asia, but the *Mictyris thailandensis* is a unique specimen. Unlike its cousins, who will march in armies together, this crab is a loner. It prefers to spend most of its time burrowed underground, emerging only during low tide, particularly on sunny days, to bask alone before digging back into the sand with a corkscrew-like motion.

9. Mangrove murex
Chicoreus capucinus

For the murex, the mangrove roots are a slow motion feast. These large snails are voracious eaters, feeding on barnacles, clams, and mussels that nest in the mangrove roots. To puncture armored prey, the murex secretes acid and bores holes into the shells of mollusks, then sucks out the soft meat inside.

10. Black-blotched porcupinefish
Diodon liturosus

The black-blotched porcupinefish lives up to its terrestrial namesake. When threatened, it will ingest water and puff its body into a spiky ball of sharp spines. It has another defense mechanism, too—this fish's flesh is poisonous.

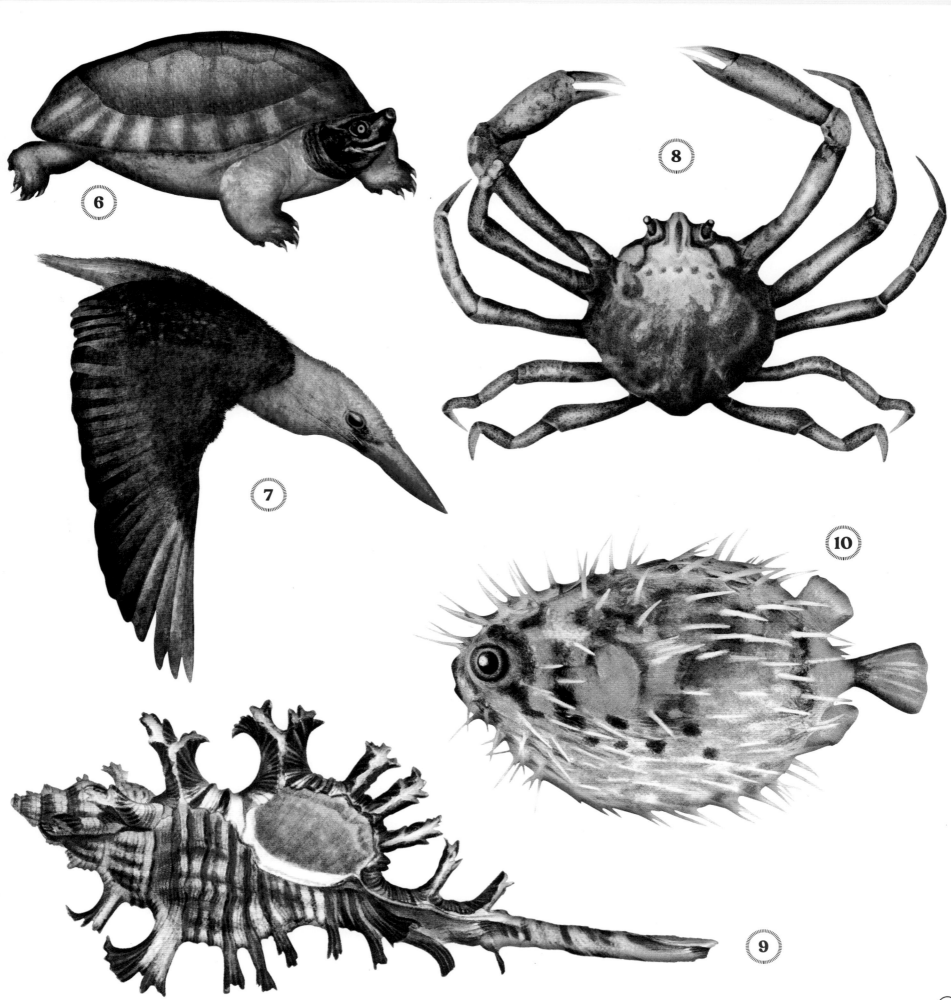

ESTUARIES

The St. Lawrence River gushes northward from North America's Great Lakes.

It passes the Canadian cities of Montreal and Quebec, and fans out to meet the cold salt water of the Gulf of St. Lawrence, a 91,000-square-mile inland sea flushed cold with Arctic currents. Where the river and the gulf meet is the world's largest estuary.

On the shores that surround this seaway are pine-covered cliffs. Craggy islands dot the icy blue waters. Beneath the surface, a vast ecosystem teems with life of all sizes, from tiny, silvery fish to blue whales, the largest mammals on Earth. Many species of whale visit here throughout the year, venturing from the Gulf past the Pointe-des-Monts, where the basin starts to narrow into an estuary. The currents in these narrower waters make for an ideal environment for krill and small forage fish called capelin, which fit nicely in the hungry filter-feeding mouths of baleen whales.

For millennia, humans have lived here, too. The Iroquois settled along the shores of this estuary long before Europeans arrived in the 1500s. In the centuries that followed, French and, later, British colonizers built cities along the river.

By the 1800s, the estuary was the main conduit for North America's timber trade. Today more than 140 million tons of cargo ship travel along the seaway of which the St. Lawrence is the heart. If the region around the river were its own country, it would be the world's third-largest economy, producing $6 trillion in annual economic activity.

That economic success comes at a cost. Pollution from industry along the river causes many problems. For example, elevated levels of toxic compounds in belugas cause cancer and hurt calves in the womb. But the bigger risk to the biodiversity in this region is climate change. Melting Arctic ice is weakening the Labrador Current, which flows south from Greenland. Without that cold water to flush out the gulf, warm water from the northward flowing Gulf Stream is raising temperatures here and bringing water with significantly less oxygen. Scientists fear that what happens next could be a domino effect, where smaller species of fish die out and provide less food for big whales.

1. Three-spined stickleback

Gasterosteus aculeatus

As its name implies, this 2-inch-long silvery fish grows three sharp spines in front of its dorsal fin. Males sometimes develop reddish bellies, are hardy, and can survive severe changes in salinity, making them well-adapted to the brackish waters where the gulf and river meet.

2. Bald eagle

Haliaeetus leucocephalus

With a maximum wingspan of more than 6.5 feet, the bald eagle is a fearsome predator from above the estuary's cold waters. The eagle's razor-sharp four-toed talons are specially adapted to have special bumps called spicules that help grip a squirming fish in flight.

3. Black tern

Chlidonias niger

The black tern changes its diet based on the season. In its mating grounds during springtime, these birds feast on insects and small mollusks. But come winter, when these birds migrate, they swoop down and pluck small fish from the water.

4. Blanding's turtle

Emydoidea blandingii

Juvenile Blanding's turtles stay close to the shallow waters, but live long lives. Their shells fully harden at five years old. By twelve, males reach sexual maturity, while females normally wait until eighteen years old to breed. In the wild, these reptiles can live more than seventy years.

5. Pumpkinseed

Lepomis gibbosus

The pumpkinseed gets its name from its greenish-brown spotted coloring, which looks a bit like the roasted autumnal snack. The *Lepomis gibbosus* is among the most common species in the North American sunfish family. That's reflected in its multitude of other nicknames, including pond perche, punkie, sunny, and kivver.

Species that live in
ESTUARIES

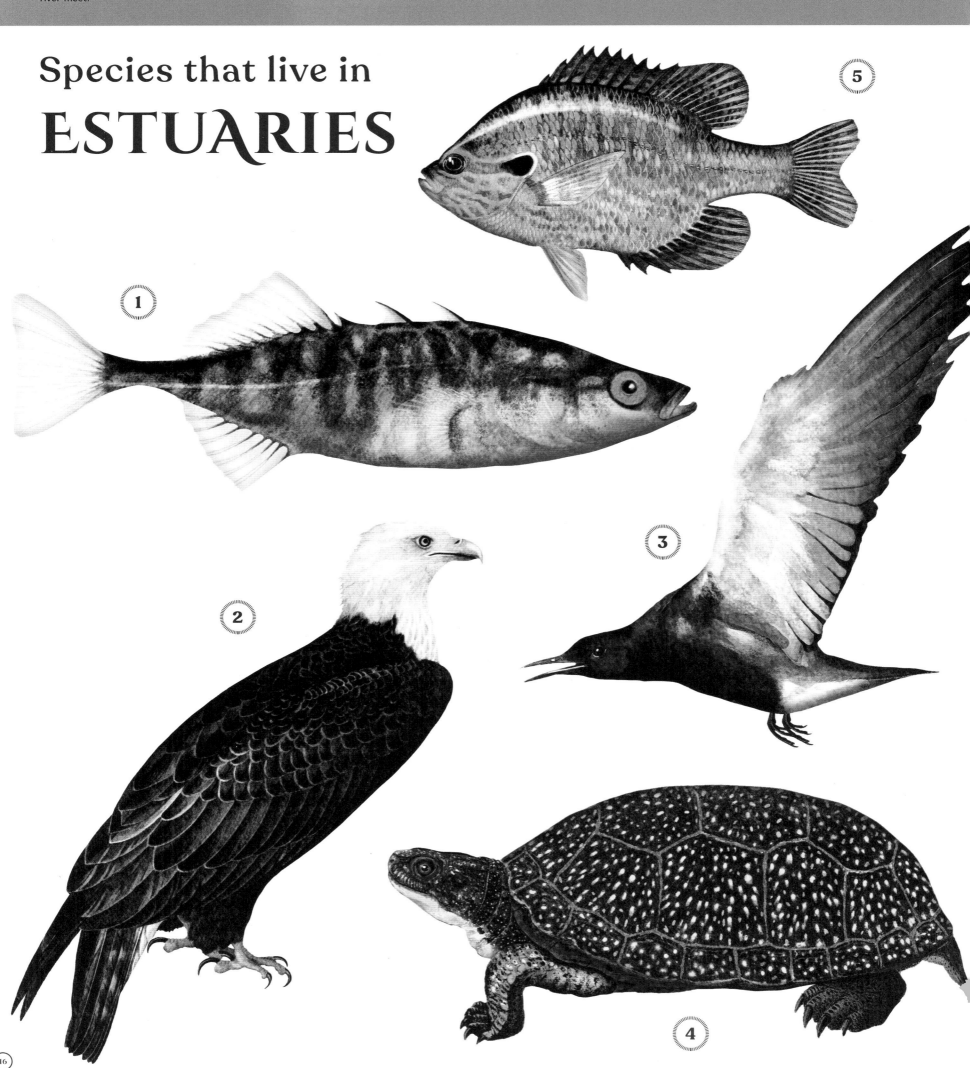

6. Longnose gar
Lepisosteus osseus

The longnose gar is an ancient fish whose slender, torpedolike bodies make them able hunters. These fish, while often caught by humans, play a vital role in ecosystems as critical predators whose voracious appetites help keep the populations of smaller fish in check.

7. Smallmouth bass
Micropterus dolomieu

For smallmouth bass, the males are the caretakers of the young. During mating, a female bass may spawn with multiple males. But the male will stay and guard the nest of eggs, which take up to a week to hatch, and then guard the juveniles until they are old enough to go off on their own.

8. Beluga
Delphinapterus leucas

The beluga is the signature animal in the St. Lawrence estuary. Its long, white body can be easily spotted near the surface. Also called a white whale, their rounded head is called a melon and allows the mammal to navigate and find prey using echolocation.

9. Hooded seal
Cystophora cristata

The hooded seal is a large, blubbery mammal with one very distinctive feature. Males have nasal sacs they inflate when threatened or attracting a mate. The sac hangs flaccidly in front of its mouth when deflated. But, inflated, the organ forms a reddish bulb that nearly doubles the size of the seal's head.

A unique ecosystem

In the middle of the Gulf of St. Lawrence sits Anticosti Island, a roughly 3,000-square-mile strip of land. Along the shores of this craggy, forested island are an estimated 400 aging shipwrecks. The rusting, dilapidated hulls of ships that ran aground on these treacherous shorelines now form a nesting spot for various species of birds, which build colonies in the broken vessels.

KELP FORESTS

Bubbles clear around your scuba mask, and you find you're in a dense, dark forest of giant kelp off California's mainland, where it's cool and shady.

These aquatic sequoias can climb higher than some trees—up to 27 feet from a rocky seabed—and like a forest on land, this ecosystem is dense with life: more than 1,000 species call it home.

The thick canopy of kelp offers protection to baby fish and crustaceans, while the stipes and blades of the kelp provide nutritious salad to a host of herbivores and omnivores.

These are hunting grounds, too. For decades,

humans were the top predator, poaching sea otters for their fur. The effect was devastating. Reducing the otter population threw the rest of the food chain into disarray. The otters have since made a comeback, but in the absence of their otter predators, purple sea urchins boomed. That's a big problem. Urchins can swarm, almost like locusts, feeding on kelp and upsetting the ecosystem. That creates barrens at the bottom. Other predators—like the sunflower sea star—have stepped in to help the otters feed on the urchins. But as global warming disrupts virtually every natural balance, these sea stars have been unable to perform their usual function.

In the areas where urchins haven't decimated the forest, life is abundant at the bottom.

Reddish-pink California spiny lobsters, notable for their lack of claws, peer out from under rock crevices, while red abalone cling to higher rocks. These hardy little snails form a vital link in the food chain here. Bright orange garibaldi dart between the kelp hunting for the abalone and urchins, joined by sea otters who dive down from the surface seeking the same prey, grabbing them with their paws, and bringing them to the surface for a crunchy meal.

1. California spiny lobster
Panulirus interruptus

The California spiny lobster typically grows about 12 inches long and feeds on all sorts of little mollusks, including the purple sea urchins, providing important protection to the kelp on which urchins prey. Unlike the Maine lobsters people often eat, spiny lobsters have no claws and use all five pairs of legs for walking.

2. Purple sea urchin
Strongylocentrotus purpuratus

The purple sea urchin looks like a spiky pincushion, with a body typically no longer than 4 inches in width. Its barbs protect it against predators and catch passing algae as a snack for these hungry urchins, whose appetite and hardiness make them significant threats to kelp forests.

3. Common bottlenose dolphin
Tursiops truncatus

Also known as Atlantic bottlenose dolphins, they live in groups called pods, hunting and playing together. These mammals communicate using high-frequency echolocation, which sounds like loud clicks and whistles. Each dolphin is believed to have their own, unique voice.

4. Sunflower sea star
Pycnopodia helianthoides

The sunflower sea star is the largest sea star in the world and can grow up to two dozen arms. If attacked, the sunflower sea star can shed one of its arms and release a chemical that alerts fellow stars in the area to be on guard. Losing an arm is no problem—they grow back.

Species that live in
KELP FORESTS

A unique ecosystem

The Channel Islands offer a warm, subtropical environment. But the larger of the islands, the 96-square-mile Santa Cruz Island, has tall mountains that create a microclimate in its central valley. Unlike most of the area, this valley will experience freezing temperatures during most winters and higher than average summer heat.

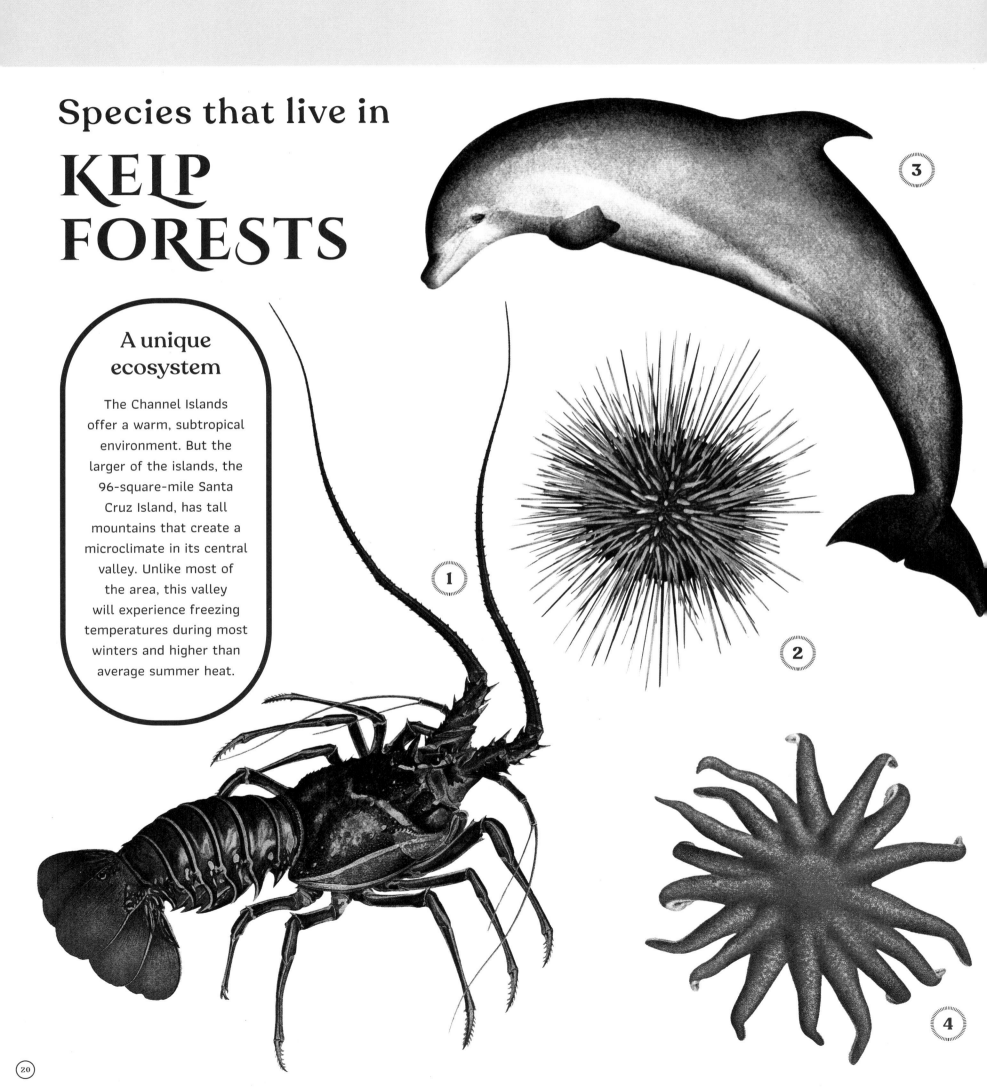

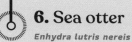

5. Giant sea bass
Stereolepis gigas

Despite its name, the giant sea bass isn't a sea bass, which belongs to the Serranidae family. It's actually more closely related to the wreckfish, from the Polyprionidae family. But it is huge. These fish can grow up to 8 feet long, weigh more than 550 pounds, and can live as long as some humans, with scientists estimating some exceeding a century in age.

6. Sea otter
Enhydra lutris nereis

Sea otters are slick, furry mammals who spend their days swimming through the kelp forests like an all-you-can-eat buffet of snails, scallops, and sea urchins. When they aren't hunting, they can be tender mothers. For the first six months of life, mother otters float with their pups on their bellies, nursing them with milk.

7. Garibaldi
Hypsypops rubicundus

The bright orange of adult garibaldi stands out, which is why they hide in kelp forests for protection from predators. But it also means that males need to go the extra mile to impress females. To attract a mate, males will swim in circles and create loud thumping sounds by clicking together big, special teeth in the back of their mouths to demonstrate how tough they are.

8. Red abalone
Haliotis rufescens

The red abalone gets its name from its brick-red shell. It's the biggest of all abalones, and, as it ages, it forms three to five holes on its shell to breathe and push out waste. A strict vegetarian, the red abalone crawls over algae and kelp and eats using its tiny, rasplike teeth.

9. Northern elephant seal
Mirounga angustirostris

The northern elephant seal spends most of its time in the water, devouring everything from shellfish to sharks to octopuses. But for three months out of the year, these blubbery giants, which can grow more than 4 yards long, and live on land to mate while on a complete fast.

SEAGRASS MEADOWS

I n one of the hottest parts of the world lies a paradise with crystal blue waters, carpeted with green seagrass meadows.

Dozens of small, sandy islands peek above the waterline, surrounded by vast, shallow waters that teem with life. This is Wadi el Gemal National Park, a large underwater platform found on the western shore of the Red Sea.

The climate of the Red Sea is hot and arid, with little rainfall and a high evaporation rate, and so—with no rivers draining into it either—the water has more salt and warmer temperatures than other aquatic habitats. These conditions may not seem, at first glance, to offer a hospitable environment for plants and animals to thrive.

However, occasionally, the region will experience very heavy rains, and then, deep valleys on the surrounding coastland, called wadis, are flooded by runoff water and dump fresh water

and sediment into the sea. These flash floods provide nutrients for the seagrass meadows that grow in sheltered, shallow areas close to the shore, which in turn offer a home to countless animals. The protective grasses and gentle currents of the seagrass meadows make them the perfect nursery for juvenile fish, who hide in the grasses, and also

corals, which form a ribbon of 26 separate seagrass meadows along the coastline. More than 153 different fish species are found here. The seagrass meadow itself is made of up to a dozen different species, which grow together in tangled harmony.

The mood here in the meadows is calm, as dugongs gently graze the seabed and green turtles nibble at the grasses. But while it may seem a paradise of serenity, this precious ecosystem is precariously close to destruction

because of pollution and rising temperatures. This region is also in the midst of a massive transformation as the government in Egypt seeks to transform the shoreline into an oasis of wealthy tourist attractions. There is still so much to learn about Wadi El Gemal's seagrass meadows, so we need to act fast to protect these nurseries of the coral reefs.

1. Collector urchin

Tripneustes gratilla

These little pincushions get the name "collector urchin" from the way their spines pick up debris as they inch along the meadow floor. *Tripneustes gratilla* are common and spawn twice a year, producing as many as 2 million eggs per clutch.

2. Red sea squirt

Halocynthia papillosa

This sea squirt often grows off rocks and develops a dark brick-like coloring. It is a suspension feeder that sates itself by gathering tiny bits of organic material from the water around it.

3. Rabbitfish

Siganus rivulatus

This is no gentle, cottontailed mammal. Quite the opposite: the rabbitfish bears long, slender spines on its back that contain venom. If a person is stung, the pain is powerful, but luckily not life-threatening.

4. Whitemargin unicornfish

Naso annulatus

The long horn that grows from the whitemargin unicornfish's head is a mystery. It's not used for defense. Instead it relies on blades near the base of its tail to ward off rivals or predators.

5. Lionfish

Pterois miles

Like the rabbitfish, the lionfish is covered in long, quill-like venomous spines. Like the big cat it's named after, this fish is dangerous to humans. A sting from its body can cause nausea, dizziness, paralysis, and even death.

Species that live in
SEAGRASS MEADOWS

6. Jayakar's seahorse
Hippocampus jayakari

Jayakar's seahorse hides among the vegetation in the bank. These seahorses grow up to 5.5 inches long. To reproduce, the female deposits eggs in a male's brood pouch, an organ located on his tail. The male will then fertilize the eggs and carry them until they hatch.

7. Humphead wrasse
Cheilinus undulatus

The king of fish in this region is the humphead wrasse—the males can grow to more than 6.5 feet long. The giant wrasse has thick, fleshy lips and can even eat poisonous creatures, like boxfishes, and crown-of-thorns starfish.

8. Dugong
Dugong dugon

Despite its huge size, the dugong lives entirely on seagrass—it can consume up to 88 pounds a day! Popularly known as sea cows, but called *Dugong dugon* by scientists, these grazing beasts leave a sandy trail behind them as they drift along the meadow bed, ripping up the grasses by the roots.

9. Purple tang
Zebrasoma xanthurum

The purple tang is a beautifully patterned fish, with a dark purple body and yellow tail— that sometimes leads it to being called a yellowtail tang. And this is a fish that likes its greens! These creatures feed on marine algae.

10. Green turtle
Chelonia mydas

Turtles such as *Chelonia mydas* are vital to the health of the seagrass beds. As they graze, they "mow" the grasses, which stimulates growth, and as they digest the food, they poo nutrients back into the meadow, providing it with food.

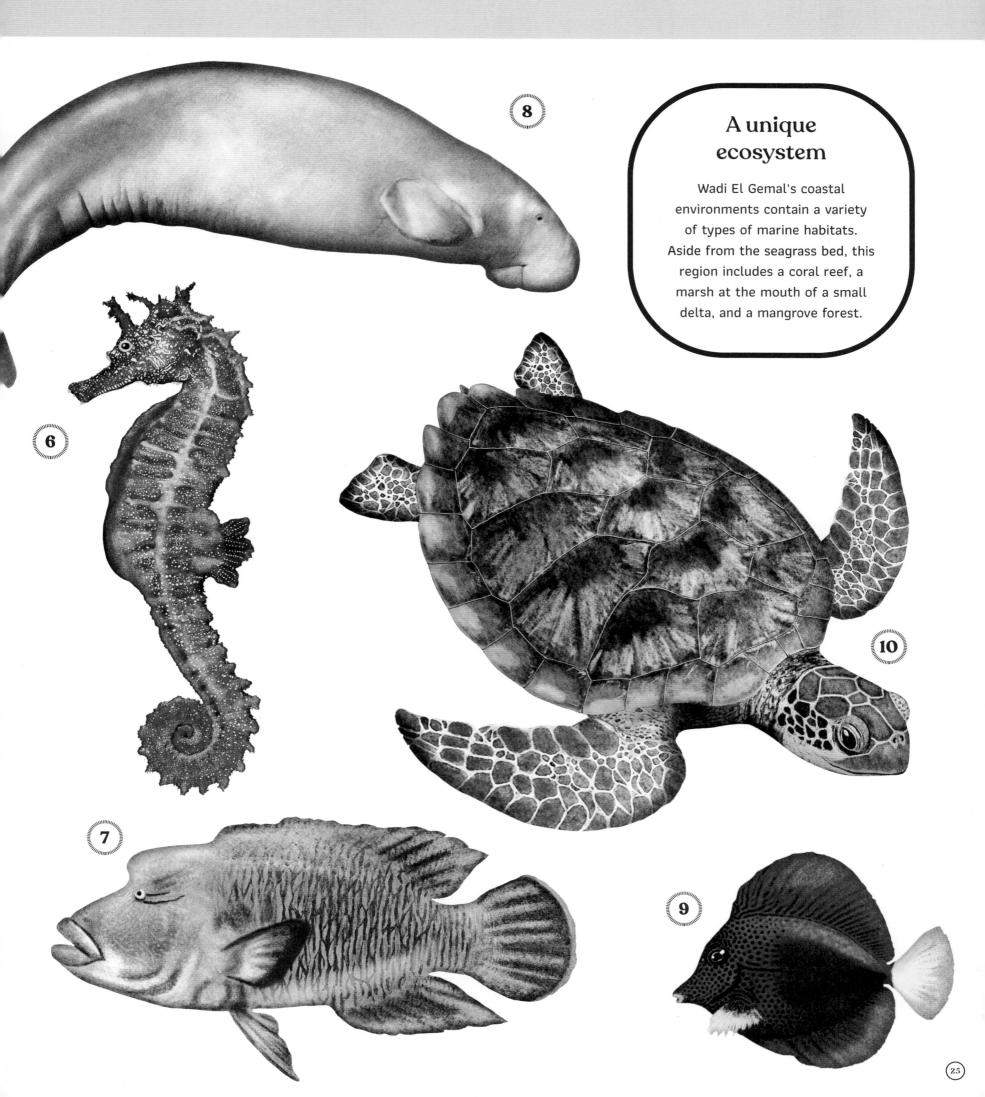

A unique ecosystem

Wadi El Gemal's coastal environments contain a variety of types of marine habitats. Aside from the seagrass bed, this region includes a coral reef, a marsh at the mouth of a small delta, and a mangrove forest.

25

CORAL REEFS

The Great Barrier Reef is an underwater metropolis. Located off Australia's northeast coast, this sprawling ecosystem is composed of 3,000 individual reefs and 1,000 islands, spanning more than 135,000 square miles.

Like the great cities of the world, the Great Barrier Reef is a dense and diverse urban landscape. More than 600 species of coral call this vast community home. Through your goggles, you can see a boundless cornucopia of color. Ivory-beige staghorn coral. Scarlet branch coral. Mustardy elkhorn coral. Mauve cauliflower coral. Pinkish-white organ pipe coral the shape of an autumnal bunch of chrysanthemums.

Corals may look like plants or rocks. But they're actually animals. Tiny creatures called polyps suck calcium carbonate—better known as limestone—from the seawater and build a hard skeleton to protect their soft, fragile bodies. This

skeleton is what you see and know as
coral.

Polyps' skeletal architecture attracts many other vibrant
creatures. Pink, white and orange anemones nestle their soft,
squishy bodies between the jagged corals, drawing anemonefish
that hide, unscathed, in the stinging tentacles. Blue sea slugs—
tiny yet otherworldly creatures—hover above the seabed.
Hunters find a feast in this environment. Blue-barred parrotfish
eye the reef for algae, while great hammerhead sharks

eye the parrotfish, turning the predator to prey. The coral itself
is food for crown-of-thorns starfish that crawl over and crunch
the skeletal structures.

Hungry, invasive starfish are the least of the reefs' worries
these days. Hotter, more acidic oceans—the result of burning
coal and other fossil fuels mined in Australia and elsewhere—
are killing corals, leaving them bleached white and lifeless. So
far, particularly hot years have been so devastating scientists
compare the damage to that of a giant wildfire. In 2016, 30 percent

of the reef's coral died off. In
2017, another year of record-
high temperatures, another 20 percent died off. That
means close to half the reef disappeared in just two years.

There is hope to reverse the trend. Scientists are
researching ways to engineer safer conditions and encourage
new coral growth. But the fate of this majestic ecosystem likely
rests in humans stopping the pollution from power plants,
factories and cars which produce planet-heating gases.

1. Cauliflower coral
Pocillopora damicornis

The cauliflower coral, also known as lace coral, is one of the most widespread reef-building corals in the world. At a moment when pollution from humans is changing the oceans and killing corals, research shows these cauliflower corals have extra strong immune systems. That makes them resilient and strong even as the environment around them changes.

2. Sea butterfly
Diacavolinia longirostris

The sea butterfly is also known by the name pteropod, which mashes together the Greek words for *fly* and *foot*. That may sound like an oxymoron, but these little sea snails, which are less than a centimetre long, can spread the slug-like foot that usually crawls along the bottom into translucent wings that allow it to swim freely.

3. Great hammerhead shark
Sphyrna mokarran

The great hammerhead shark is the largest of nine species of hammerhead sharks, with some individuals growing about 20 feet long. Its T-shaped head is equipped with electrical receptors that detect prey—anything from squids to stingrays to other sharks—even if its meal is hiding under the sand on the seafloor.

4. Barrier Reef anemonefish
Amphiprion akindynos

You found Nemo! The Barrier Reef anemonefish is commonly mistaken for a clownfish, and served as the inspiration for Pixar's *Finding Nemo*. These fish live among the tentacles of anemones, but evade their sting with a special mucus that protects the fish.

Species that live in
CORAL REEFS

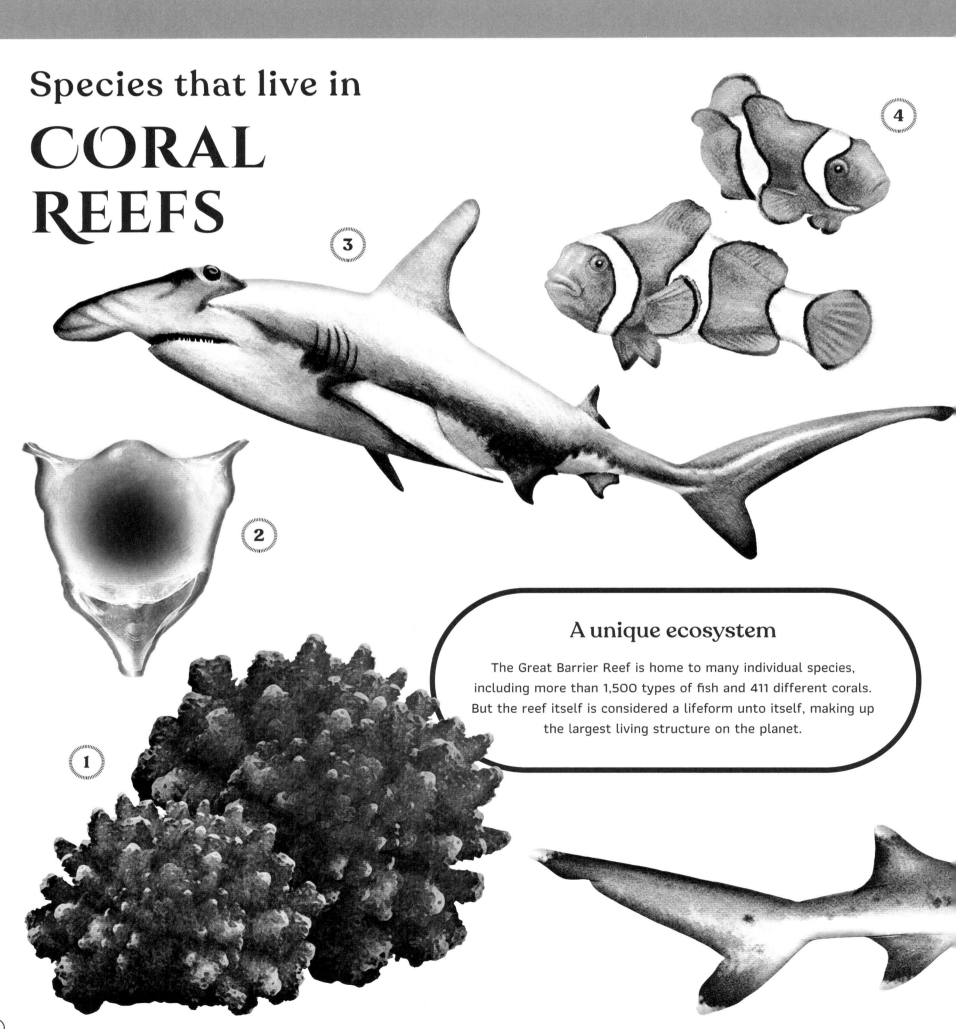

A unique ecosystem

The Great Barrier Reef is home to many individual species, including more than 1,500 types of fish and 411 different corals. But the reef itself is considered a lifeform unto itself, making up the largest living structure on the planet.

5. Giant clam

Tridacna gigas

The giant clam can grow more than 5 feet, but eats like most bivalve mollusks, by filtering tiny plankton through its ctenidia, or gills. Yet these clams picked up a trick from its coral neighbors. On its body, the giant clam grows microscopic algae that, like plants, feeds on sunlight. That algae provides the bulk of the clam's nutrients—so much so that, left in a dark place without sunlight, the clam will die.

6. Blue-barred parrotfish

Scarus ghobban

The blue-barred parrotfish gets its name from its distinct, beak-like teeth, which are incredibly hard and continually grow, replacing older, worn teeth. This makes it possible for the fish to crunch through rock-hard coral as easy as biting into a cookie. The parrotfish's diet of coral also has an added benefit to beachgoers: They poo out soft white sand.

7. Whitetip reef shark

Triaenodon obesus

The whitetip reef shark may look scary, especially at a full size reaching around 5 feet long. These nocturnal fish like to slumber all day and come out at night to feed on small fish in reefs and caves. But they're known to be gentle with humans—so much so that scientists report feeding the sharks by hand.

8. Blue sea slug

Glaucus atlanticus

The blue sea slug is another dazzling mollusk whose unique look garners many common names: blue dragon, blue swallow, blue angel. But these little creatures, which grow to less than 1 inch in length, have an impressive talent: They feed on giant, poisonous jellyfish and store their stinging venom for later, to defend themselves from predators.

9. Crown-of-thorns starfish

Acanthaster planci

The crown-of-thorns starfish are dangerous partners for humans in destroying reefs. These prickly starfish feast on corals by pushing their stomachs through their mouths and digesting soft tissue off the coral's skeleton. Coupled with pollution from humans, crown-of-thorns starfish pose a serious threat to corals.

Conservation efforts

Pollution and ocean acidification are killing the reef at an unprecedented speed. But scientists and environmentalists are fighting back. In 2018, they launched the largest-ever project to regenerate corals by breeding the animals in areas where the reef had died out.

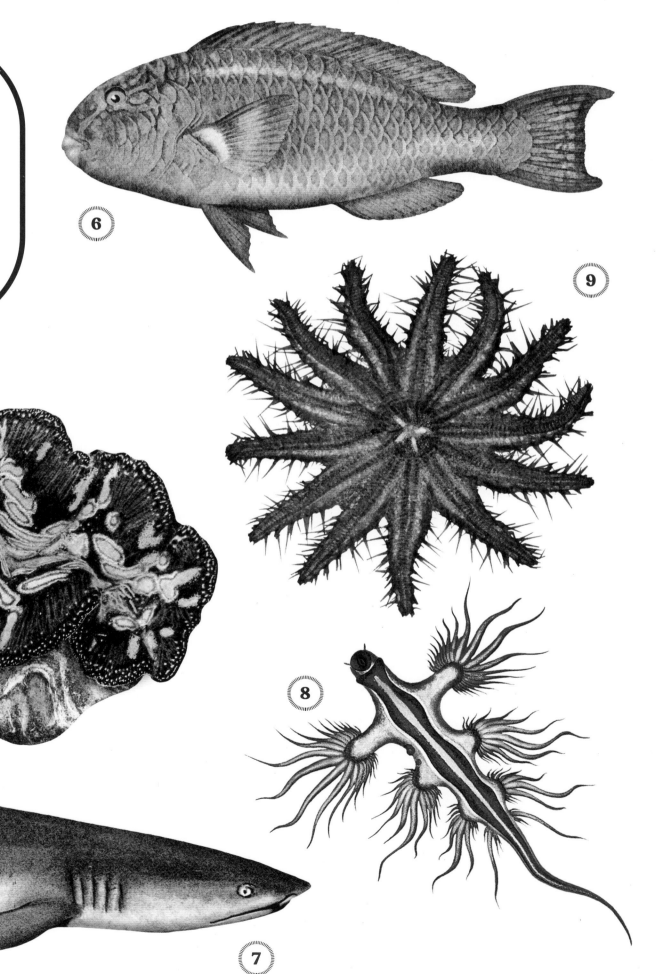

OYSTER REEFS

Long before main roads, beachfront suburban houses, and boats lined the United States' densely populated Eastern Seaboard, the muddy waters of this coast contained an oyster empire.

Billions upon billions of bivalves blossomed like boundless fields of greyish-brown stones, clumped together in the cool muck.

For thousands of years, oysters served as a staple for human diets. The first humans settled here more than 12,000 years ago. When Ice Age glaciers retreated roughly 3,000 years ago, the warm, shallow bay we now know as the Chesapeake Bay became a perfect breeding ground for the great eastern oyster. By the early 1800s, roughly 200 years after European colonizers

violently drove the Indigenous peoples who lived here away and industrialized the waterfront, fishers in Maryland and Virginia, the two biggest states on the bay, were hauling over a million bushels of oysters per year.

Between 1890 and 1930, oyster harvests plummeted by nearly two thirds. Part of the problem was overfishing.

But another issue was the spread of two parasite diseases which thrive in saltier water, made worse by drought years, when there isn't enough fresh rainwater to balance the salty ocean water. At one point, in the 1950s, the diseases wiped out nearly 90 percent of the oyster population in the bay. The harvests only declined from there.

Hungry humans were hardly the only ones to suffer from losing oysters. Bivalves are famous for filtering the water around them, "vacuuming" or cleaning toxins and pollutants,

while their crevices offer safety from predators to sponges, worms, crabs, and baby fish.

In the early 2000s, oysters started to make a comeback, thanks in part to humans who decided to replenish the population their ancestors helped destroy. Farmers began growing oysters in coastal beds. And conservationists started seeding oysters throughout the bay in hopes the bivalves would help clean up pollution and encourage wild animals and plant life to return.

1. Feather blenny

Hypsoblennius hentz

The feather blenny is named for the feathery flap of skin on its head, which it uses to detect activity in the water around it. Growing to around 4 inches, this fish is highly territorial and will ward off intruders, charging at much bigger fish.

2. Blue mussel

Mytilus edulis

The blue mussel is one of the most common bivalves in the world, with its blackish-navy shells showing up on beaches—and garlic and butter drizzled dinner plates—all over the world. These shellfish can survive in a wide range of temperatures, suggesting they may be a hardy species as climate change becomes worse.

3. Daggerblade grass shrimp

Palaemonetes pugio

The tiny, translucent daggerblade grass shrimp is a common source of food for fish and other crustaceans in the oyster reef. But that doesn't mean these yellow-and-brown spotted decapods go down without a fight. This shrimp is known to jab its predators with the sharp tip of its head, or rostrum.

4. Naked goby

Gobiosoma bosc

Don't worry, there's no need to look away from the naked goby. This fish sports a beautiful striped pattern, and its skin is smooth to touch. Unlike many fish, this bottom feeder, which grows only around 1 inch long, is "naked" because it has no scales. The species is dependent on oysters to reproduce as female lays her eggs in empty oyster shells.

Species that live in
OYSTER REEFS

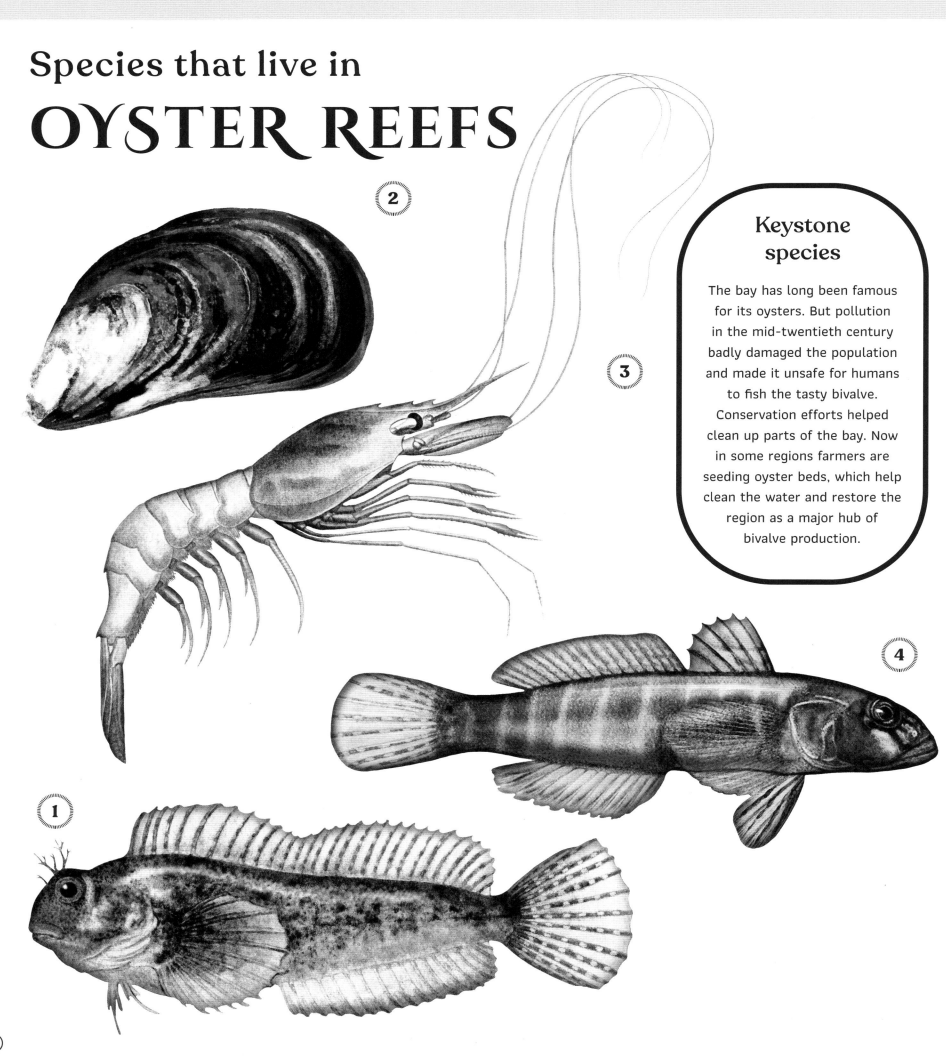

Keystone species

The bay has long been famous for its oysters. But pollution in the mid-twentieth century badly damaged the population and made it unsafe for humans to fish the tasty bivalve. Conservation efforts helped clean up parts of the bay. Now in some regions farmers are seeding oyster beds, which help clean the water and restore the region as a major hub of bivalve production.

5. Blackfish
Tautoga onitis

The blackfish, or tautog, has powerful, rounded canine teeth in the front of its mouth that easily crunch through crabs, shellfish, and barnacles. When it isn't feeding, it will find a hole in the oyster reef and go to sleep on its sides, often laying so flat and still predators can't see them.

6. Oyster toadfish
Opsanus tau

The oyster toadfish looks like a fierce, olive-colored blob with a big mouth and fleshy lips. This bottom feeder, who normally preys on mollusks and small crustaceans and can grow more than 15 inches long, can vibrate its swim bladder to create a deep, croak-like grunting sound to ward off predators and attract mates.

7. Atlantic oyster drill
Urosalpinx cinerea

The Atlantic oyster drill may look small and innocent, but these sea snails are fearsome predators. They bore tiny holes in baby oysters, softening their shells with an acidic secretion and filing into them with a serrated organ called a radula to then feast on the soft flesh inside.

8. Eastern oyster
Crassostrea virginica

The mighty eastern oyster clusters in these reefs, helping to clean the water and creating habitats for other life with their bunches of shells. These bivalves can survive all over the eastern coast of North America in part because, when the water temperatures drop close to freezing, they can close their shells and stay shut until the water warms again.

9. Flatworm
Stylochus ellipticus

One of the eastern oyster's biggest threats comes from the flatworm. The predatory flatworm gorges on the oyster's fleshy body, hampering conservation efforts to bolster oyster populations in the Chesapeake Bay.

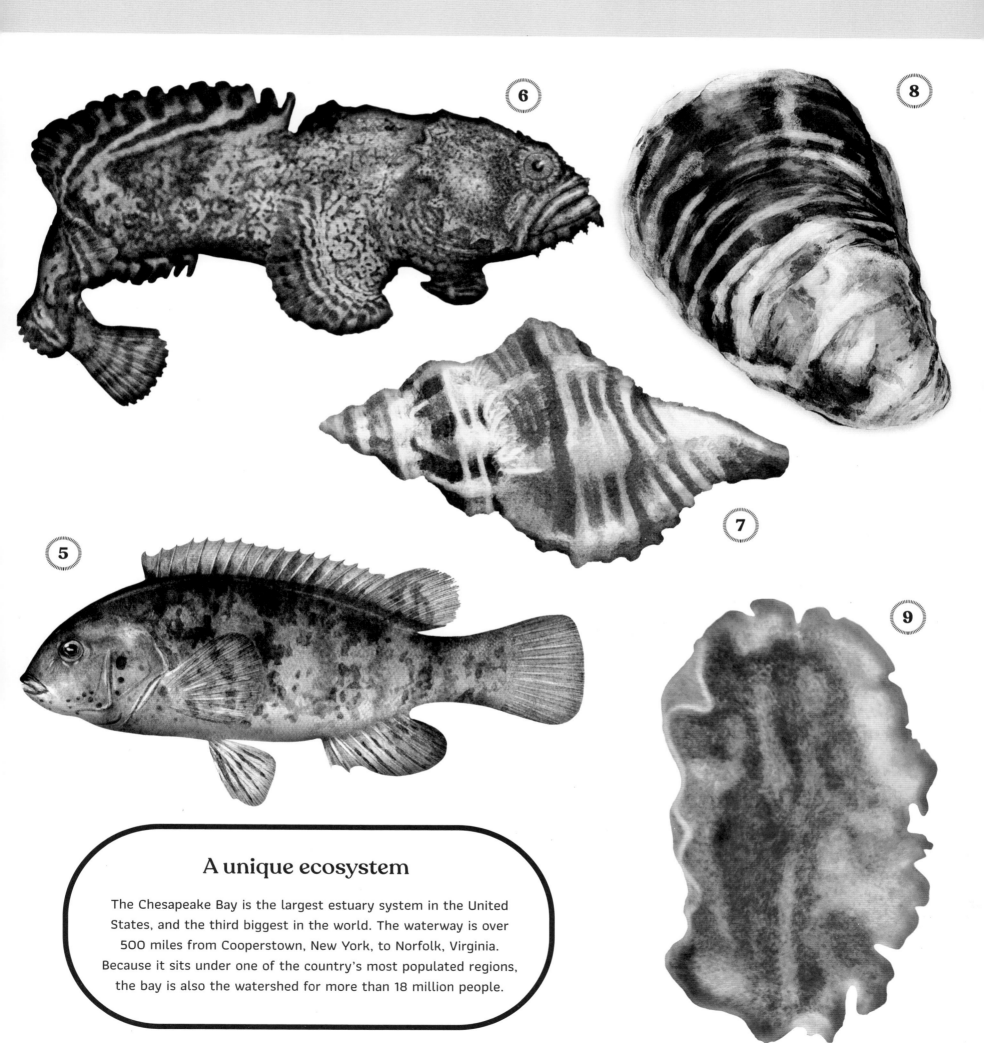

A unique ecosystem

The Chesapeake Bay is the largest estuary system in the United States, and the third biggest in the world. The waterway is over 500 miles from Cooperstown, New York, to Norfolk, Virginia. Because it sits under one of the country's most populated regions, the bay is also the watershed for more than 18 million people.

OPEN WATER

Welcome to the mighty Pacific. The planet's largest ocean covers about 64 million square miles, stretching from the western shores of California to the eastern coast of China. It contains more than half the Earth's unfrozen water.

It's also the oldest of the world's five oceans. The Pacific started to form nearly 800 million years ago when the Panthalassic Ocean, an ancient superocean that existed before the continents took their current shape, began to change. Roughly 200 million years ago, the "old Pacific," as the Panthalassic is sometimes known, started to look a little more like the giant blue basin we see today.

In the 1520s, while sailing through a calm patch, the Portuguese explorer Ferdinand Magellan named this ocean the Mar Pacífico, which translates to "peaceful sea" in both Portuguese and Spanish. In reality, the Pacific was anything

but. This giant body of water included what scientists call the Ring of Fire, a 25,000-mile horseshoe-shaped ring of active volcanoes, perpetually exploding, gurgling lava, and triggering earthquakes. Yet between those violent underwater mountains, life flourished in every corner of the Pacific.

Near the Pacific's placid surface floated phytoplankton, microscopic plantlike organisms that feed on sunlight. On seafloors grew verdant forests of kelp and seaweed on which crabs and small fish grazed. A food chain formed. The crabs and small fish fed bigger fish. The bigger fish fed penguins and seals. The penguins and seals fed sharks and orcas. All the while, the biggest creature of them all, the blue whale, feasted on tiny, shrimplike krill.

Today, however, it is an ecosystem under threat. The Pacific is growing abnormally hot and more acidic as gases from humans' cars, farms, and factories create the equivalent of a stuffy winter coat around the planet.

The oceans absorb most of those gases and start to change in ways that make it harder for creatures living there to survive. Making things worse are the tons upon tons of plastic waste humans throw away every year, of which a huge amount ends up in the Pacific, threatening the oceans natural wonders.

1. Bluefin tuna
Thunnus orientalis

One of the largest ray-finned fish in the ocean, the bluefin tuna grows to 5 feet and weighs in around 130 pounds, though some as big as 10 feet and 1,000 pounds have been netted. It navigates thousands of miles through the vast waters of the Pacific Ocean with impressive strength and speed, using its muscular body to propel itself with its tail fin.

2. Giant Pacific octopus
Enteroctopus dofleini

At 110 pounds and nearly 16 feet across, the giant Pacific octopus is the world's largest species of eight-legged cephalopod. It is a cunning hunter that uses one of the animal kingdom's most sophisticated camouflage systems. It's also fast and can easily compress its legs into an aerodynamic rocket shape.

3. Great white shark
Carcharodon carcharias

The great white shark is the largest predatory fish species in the world, growing up to 20 feet in length. Its sheer size is its most powerful adaptation. An apex predator, the shark can feed on anything from fish to seals to even a sperm whale.

4. Blue whale
Balaenoptera musculus

The blue whale is the largest animal to have ever lived, bigger than any dinosaur and longer than two school buses. Despite its size, this species feeds on tiny krill, which it filters with stiff, hairlike baleen instead of teeth. Twin blowholes and superefficient lungs allow this mammal to stay underwater for long periods of time.

Species that live in
OPEN WATER

Plastic waste

The north-central Pacific contains a shameful blemish. Floating amid the ocean is a giant dump of plastic waste, known as the Great Pacific Garbage Patch. The patch resulted from the millions of tons of plastic waste humans dump in the ocean every year. Today the patch is roughly three times the size of France, and risks spreading toxic microplastics throughout the marine food chain.

5. Humpback whale
Megaptera novaeangliae

Humpback whales begin their lives in the safe, calm waters of the tropics, later traveling more than 15,000 miles to find food—krill—which can be found in the polar waters. The whale is named for the large hump on its back and is one of nature's most musical creatures, singing its complex song for 24 hours at a time.

6. Broadbill swordfish
Xiphias gladius

The broadbill swordfish swims in nearly every ocean, though close to half of those caught by fishermen are in the Pacific. These silvery hunters grow more than 13 feet long. Up to one third of their body is a long, serrated sword used to slash prey, including squid and cuttlefish.

7. Giant manta ray
Mobula birostris

Giant manta rays live up to their name, with wingspans nearly 30 feet wide and the biggest brains of any fish. These solitary creatures are super intelligent, and research suggests they can even recognize themselves in mirrors. Their mouths are specially adapted to feed on tiny zooplankton.

8. Sockeye salmon
Oncorhynchus nerka

Sockeye salmon thrive in the cold waters off of North America, where their pinkish bodies, silvery-green heads, and white bellies make them distinct. These fish feed on zooplankton and small crustaceans and are what's known as anadromous, meaning they swim from oceans up freshwater streams, where they lay eggs.

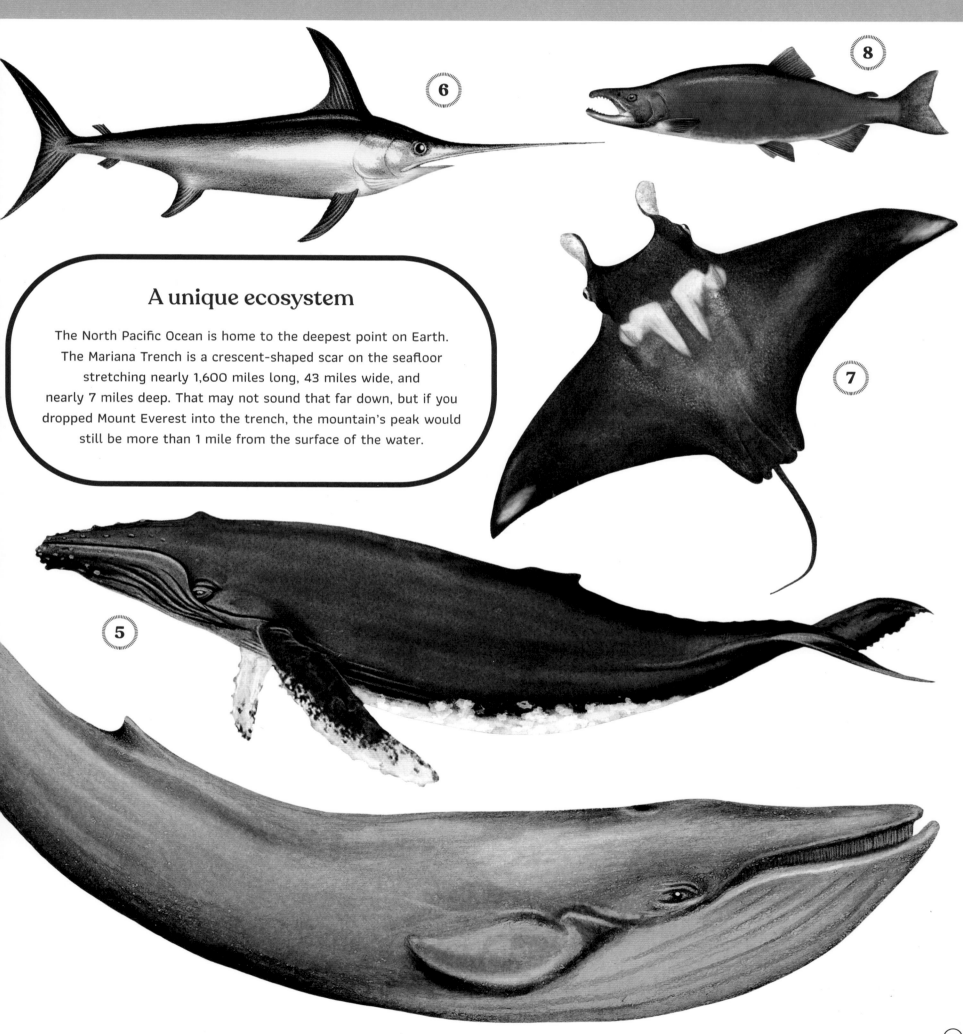

A unique ecosystem

The North Pacific Ocean is home to the deepest point on Earth. The Mariana Trench is a crescent-shaped scar on the seafloor stretching nearly 1,600 miles long, 43 miles wide, and nearly 7 miles deep. That may not sound that far down, but if you dropped Mount Everest into the trench, the mountain's peak would still be more than 1 mile from the surface of the water.

SEA ICE

In September, the end of winter in the Southern hemisphere, these vast ice floes cover an area roughly 7 million square miles off of all Antarctica's coasts. But in February's summer warmth, the sea ice contracts to hug the shoreline.

Antarctica is the only continent devoid of a human population. Its ice floes, while melting, look like giant, jagged lily pads of snow. This expanse of grey and white has no obvious vegetation. But it is anything but barren. Normally in giant colonies on land, macaroni penguins, notable for their feathery yellow brows, congregate in small groups atop the floats, resting after a hunt. Weddell seals, their bellies full of fish, gather on their own ice floes.

Beneath the bobbing sea ice, this remote and extreme ecosystem is even more diverse. Due to the tilt of the Earth's axis, Antarctica experiences six months of complete daylight

during summer and is shrouded in six months of darkness during winter. Adapted to long stretches of darkness, many creatures are pale, such as the ghostly grey Antarctic octopus, while others are virtually transparent, like Antarctic krill. These small crustaceans form the cornerstone of the food chain here, swimming in schools close to the surface. Tunicates, a diverse family of tiny invertebrates, thrive across the water column, while the salp, an inchworm-like tunicate, has a body which looks like a wiggly water toy.

The seabed is dark, rigid with rocks and stalks of brown kelp that emerge in the sunny months. At some point earlier in the season, an iceberg cleaved off one of the glaciers on shore and stabbed the bottom with a sharp edge of ice, gouging an uneven and squiggly trench as it shook free from the land. At the freshly tilled bottom, new life emerges: another species of tunicate, glass tulips, which are stationary, sprout upward. On their long stems, pale feather stars cling and climb.

The extreme seasons here belie another, more radical change unfolding: Global warming is rapidly destabilizing the glaciers and melting sea ice at a faster rate. So take a snapshot of these ice floes; they may not reoccur for long.

1. Weddell seal
Leptonychotes weddellii

Weddell seals are grey and spotted, with a blubbery body which protects its organs from the severe cold of the ocean. But their most useful adaptation is their ability to dive more than 1,600 feet and hold their breath underwater for more than an hour. That helps these mammals avoid predators, such as killer whales.

2. Antarctic octopus
Megaleledone setebos

At 35 inches in length, the Antarctic octopus is a relative giant with ghostly pale coloring. What makes this creature particularly unique is that it feeds on mollusks by drilling holes in the shells and injecting them with venomous saliva. The venom, which is still mysterious to scientists, works at colder temperatures than almost any other animal venom.

3. Antarctic midge
Belgica antarctica

The Antarctic midge is what you might call an extreme insect. It lives most of its life as a larva frozen in ice. The flightless, black-bodied adult barely breaks 6 millimeters, but it is the largest land animal on the Antarctic continent. It is so accustomed to its freezing surroundings that temperatures of 50° Fahrenheit or more can prove fatal.

4. Glass sea tulip
Pyura spinifera

The glass sea tulip grows a bulbous knob atop a stalk that stems from rocky coasts. These alien-looking creatures aren't flowers at all. They're sea squirts, or ascidians, a type of invertebrate filter feeder. This particular species develops a 12-inch-long, translucent body, earning its comparison to glass.

5. Salp
Salpa thompsoni

The salp looks like a tiny orange bean in a 1.5-inch tube of translucent jelly. Its barrel-shaped body filters cold ocean water and feeds on the tiny plankton. To move, it propels itself forward by squeezing water through its body to form a jet—simple, but effective! As the polar waters warm up, these little tunicates are traveling further and further south.

Species that live on
SEA ICE

6. Brown kelp
Macrocystis

Because Antarctica is on one of the Earth's poles, sunlight soaks the region for six months of the year. Darkness envelops the other half of the year. That makes the brown kelp particularly adept at responding to seasonal changes, leading it to grow quickly during the spring and summer months.

7. Feather star
Promachocrinus kerguelensis

Feather stars live across the Southern Ocean, including on sea ice. These whitish-mauve crinoids are cousins of sea stars and sea cucumbers, and use their feathery arms to catch and feed on plankton floating by. If one of their arms is damaged or eaten by a predator, they can grow another one.

8. Orca
Orcinus orca

This black-and-white mammal may look like the panda bear of the sea, but they're nothing like the peaceful bamboo eaters. Orcas were long known by the nickname "killer whale"—and for good reason. These dolphin relatives are highly intelligent and excellent hunters whose carnivorous diets are specific to what their families, or pods, eat.

9. Antarctic toothfish
Dissostichus mawsoni

Named after the two rows of teeth on its upper jaw, the Antarctic toothfish is the "shark" of the southern seas and can grow to a length of 5.5 feet, hungrily hunting down smaller fish and shrimp to help it survive the cold waters in which it lives. It also produces a kind of antifreeze, allowing it to survive the coldest temperatures.

10. Macaroni penguin
Eudyptes chrysolophus

The macaroni penguin sports a distinctive brow of yellow feathers and has excellent eyesight underwater. But it finds its real safety in numbers. These penguins, which grow more than 2 feet tall, live in colonies that number nearly 2.5 million—about as many people that live in Brooklyn, New York.

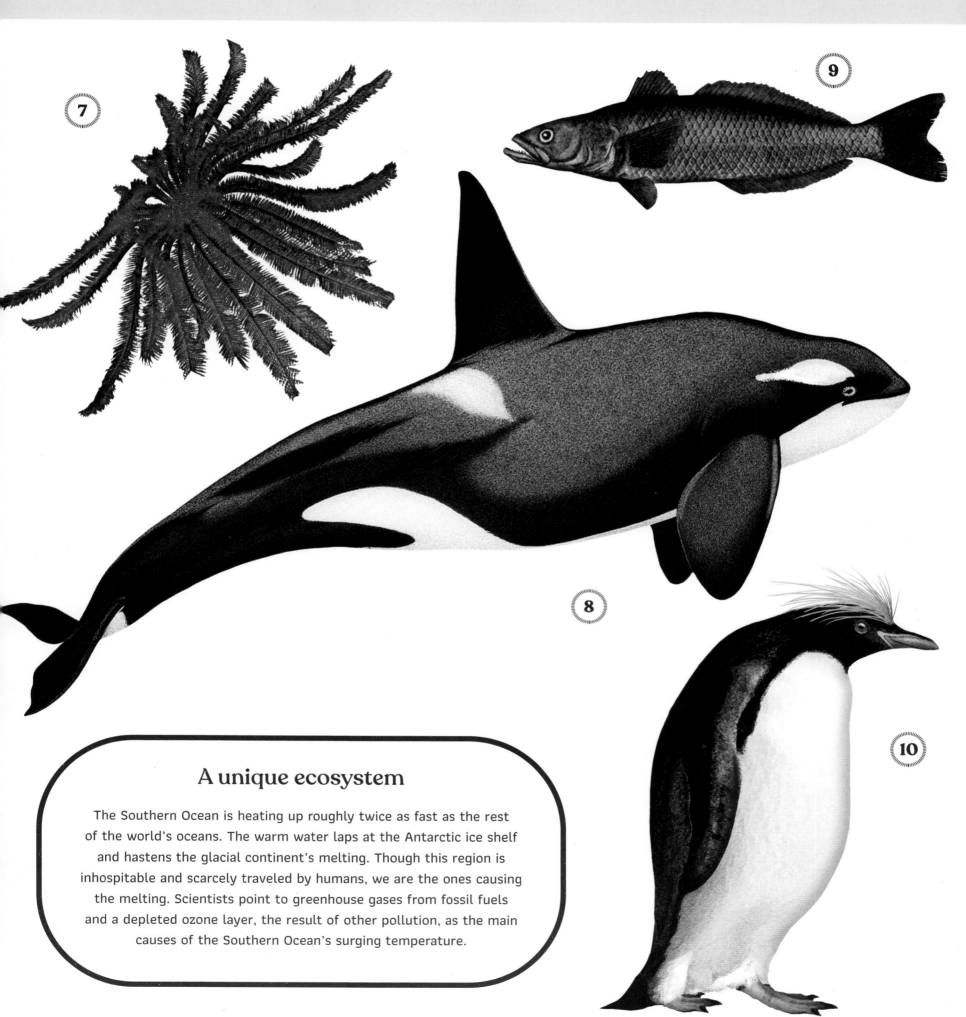

A unique ecosystem

The Southern Ocean is heating up roughly twice as fast as the rest of the world's oceans. The warm water laps at the Antarctic ice shelf and hastens the glacial continent's melting. Though this region is inhospitable and scarcely traveled by humans, we are the ones causing the melting. Scientists point to greenhouse gases from fossil fuels and a depleted ozone layer, the result of other pollution, as the main causes of the Southern Ocean's surging temperature.

SALT MARSHES

You wouldn't know it now, but this soaked and murky marsh–fed with fresh water from the river Scheldt and salt water from the North Sea–once offered one of the most prosperous farming in all of Medieval Europe.

In the 1200s, the Dutch-Flemish rulers of this area drained the swamps and farmed the rich, fertile land, creating villages known as polders. This system lasted for about two centuries.

In 1570, disaster struck the villagers who lived and farmed the drained peat. Storms brought what became known as the All Saints Flood. As many as 20,000 people died. After that, it became clear that this land belonged to the sea, and the swamps and marshes once again took hold.

Today, this area represents roughly 13 square miles of tranquil life. Common reeds and marsh grass abound, knitting the land together to fight erosion and providing

homes for birds and insects. Scurvy grass blooms with soft white blossoms. Sea lavender bursts with purple firework displays of flowers. Club rush brandish golden-brown spikelets that look something like the flails medieval warriors likely carried through these parts in earlier times.

The bramble of grasses and brush provide welcome homes to the winged inhabitants of this region. That includes bluethroats, whose marvelous males sport round

displays of bright blue and orange upper breasts and cling to the club rush stalks. These birds are hunting for insects, and rare ones call this place home, too. Sea aster mining bees come here to feed on their favorite purple flowers.

As climate change raises sea levels, such bees find fewer places to nest. That makes some humanmade structures ideal alternatives.

Not everyone is drowned out by the water. On the silty, clay banks, encrusted with rocks and veined with roots,

mollusks find cozy burrows. Sand gapers and white piddocks find safety and comfort here. They may be invisible from the surface, but the gapers are known to spit. When the pressure from the mud around them starts to squeeze too tightly, they expel water, creating some more breathing room.

Finned residents of this area include thinlip mullets, silvery little hunters who seek out common gobies for a meal.

1. White piddock
Barnea candida

The white piddock is a sharp clam with a talent for digging. With four special muscles that allow it to move its shell like an axe, it burrows into clay, peat, or soft rock. This shy and nervous animal will easily take fright and hide within its fragile shell, which doesn't completely close around its body.

2. Thinlip mullet
Chelon ramada

The life of a thinlip mullet begins at sea, where these silvery-grey fish spawn. Babies then migrate into estuaries, while adults travel in schools into marshes, lagoons, and rivers. Their tendency to travel close to the shore makes them susceptible to coastal pollution from humans.

3. Common goby
Pomatoschistus microps

Female common gobies like a male who can sing. This small, ray-finned fish lives at the bottom of the marsh, and attracts its mate by emitting a sound similar to a purring cat. The female lays the eggs in a sheltered spot, and the male watches over them until they are hatched.

4. Common sea lavender
Limonium vulgare

The common sea lavender spreads in vast meadows that turn light purple when the plants bloom. Compared to other species of the flowering herb, *Limonium vulgare* are very hardy—they can survive in both dry and wet extremes, and in the high levels of salt in the water—making them equipped to handle any tide in the marsh.

Species that live in
SALT MARSHES

Dekzand

Much of the bed of the Saeftinghe is peat, made up of millennia of decomposing plant matter. But there's an even more ancient layer of sand beneath the peat. This sandy layer, known as dekzand, is the remains of an old dune system that existed here during the last Ice Age.

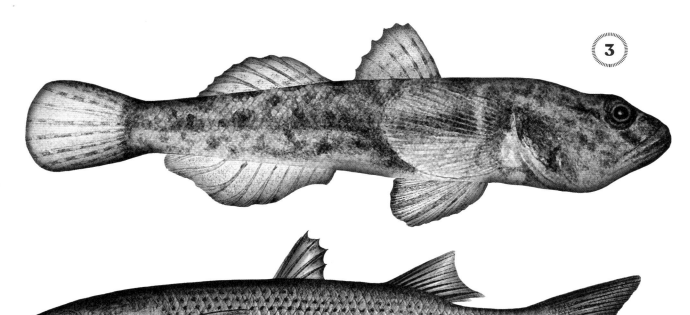

5. Sea aster mining bee
Colletes halophilus

The sea aster mining bee is a rare species of bee. These insects tend to live solitary lives feeding on pollen from marsh flowers. But the males will sometimes live with roommates, building nests in dry, sandy soil, called roosts.

6. Sea club rush
Bolboschoenus maritimus

The sea club rush form meadows on marshlands. It's easy to identify by its tall flower stems that rise above the leaves in the summertime. The stems of sea club rush are crowned with brown spikelets, like little pine cones, and make useful perches for birds.

7. Bluethroat
Luscinia svecica

The bluethroat sports a round pattern of bright blue and reddish-orange feathers on its breast and a red tail that makes for marvelous display in flight. But the bluethroat tends to spend its time skulking secretively in the tall grasses of marshlands, calling to its fellow songbirds with a chirp that goes *cheep-CHEEEEEEEEP, cheep-CHEEEEEEEEP.*

8. Sand gaper
Mya arenaria

Sand gapers are soft-shell clams that burrow into the muddy marsh floor. When the tide is out, these edible clams, sometimes called steamers or Ipswich clams, eject water high into the air to clear the pressure of mud gathering around them.

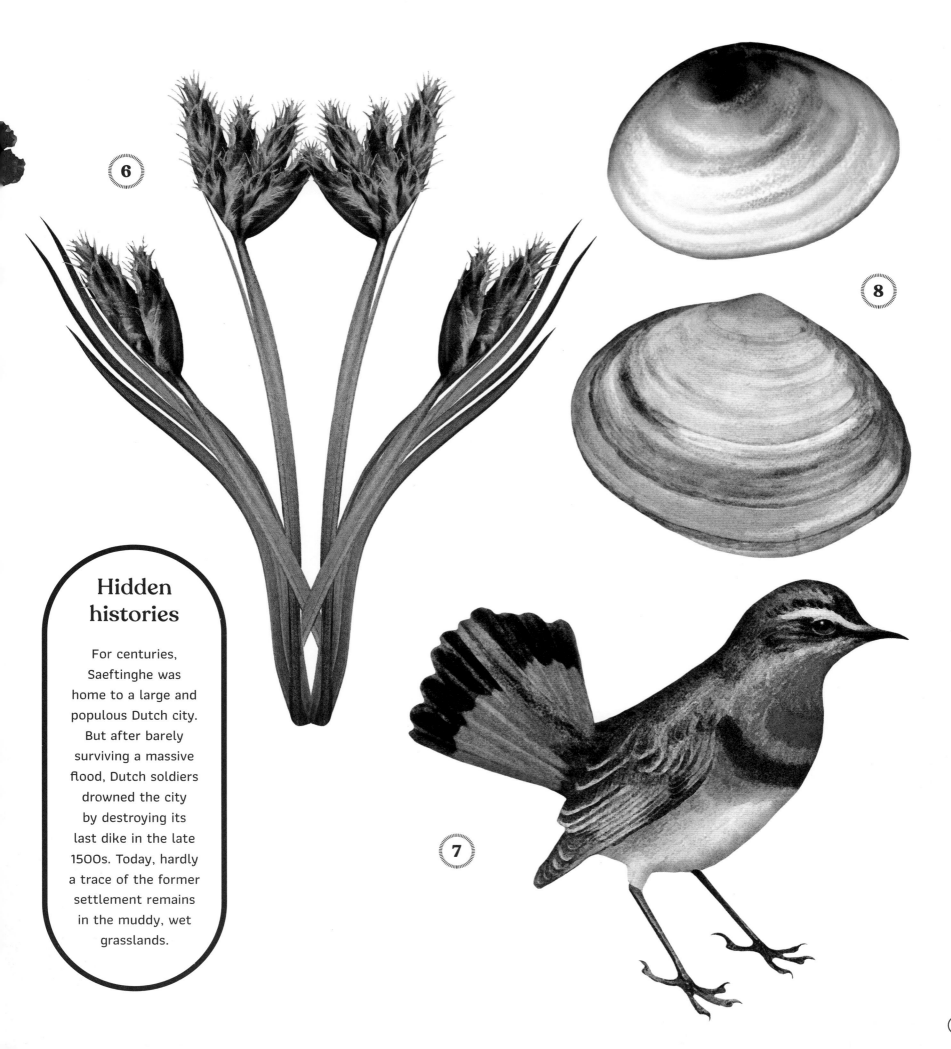

Hidden histories

For centuries, Saeftinghe was home to a large and populous Dutch city. But after barely surviving a massive flood, Dutch soldiers drowned the city by destroying its last dike in the late 1500s. Today, hardly a trace of the former settlement remains in the muddy, wet grasslands.

SLOW-MOVING FRESH WATER

From space, Lake Baikal is a waxing crescent sliver of water in the center of the Asian continent. But this is both the world's deepest and largest freshwater lake by volume and, at 12,248 square miles, the seventh-largest lake by surface area.

Sometimes called the Pearl of Siberia, Lake Baikal is 5,387 feet deep in places and holds more fresh water than all the Great Lakes of North America combined. Scientists believe it to be one of the world's oldest lakes, having formed in a continental rift some 25 million years ago.

Its ancientness and isolation from other bodies of water make it one of the most unique and diverse ecosystems on Earth, earning the nickname the Galápagos of Russia. The lake's frigid depths feature ghostly oilfish and pale-green sponges that exist nowhere else in the world. Small worms plant themselves alongside the sponges and produce tentacle-like

limbs that resemble sea anemones. Similarly otherworldly are the more than 350 species of amphipods. This lake is home to many fish species, but few are as prized or storied among humans as the Baikal sturgeon and the Arctic omul. The armored sturgeon's eggs are sold as some of the most desired caviar in Russia.

The surface has its own wonders. Jagged, pine-covered hills, small mountains, and subarctic tundra surround the lake. On the rocky shore, a bob of nerpas—the world's only seal species that lives primarily in fresh water—lounges in the sun. But there are signs of trouble, too. Toxic algae has increasingly become a problem on the lake, coating entire areas in a thick, gloopy green netting. The culprit is partly from pollution from the industrial sites along the lake's shore. But climate change is an even bigger problem. Since 1979, rising

temperatures have been linked to a 300 percent increase in algae blooms. As the region warms, the lake will freeze less, take in more water and become hotter. Conservation efforts are needed to preserve this ancient ecosystem.

1. Gammarus
Eulimnogammarus verrucosus

Lake Baikal is home to more than 350 species of amphipods—tiny, spiky crustaceans that look like a cross between a lobster and a beetle and are sometimes known as freshwater shrimp. Studies show its haemolymph, or blood, has the potential to be used for natural treatments.

2. Nerpa
Pusa sibirica

The nerpa is the world's only seal that lives primarily in fresh water. This furry mammal breaks breathing holes in the ice when the lake freezes over in the winter and uses its sharp claws, teeth, and strong rear flipper to keep the holes open until spring.

3. Sponge
Lubomirskia baikalensis

The *Lubomirskia baikalensis* grows like asparagus stalks in frigid water. They're green, too. That's because microalgae covers these species of freshwater sponges and helps fuel their growth.

4. Baikal sturgeon
Acipenser baerii baicalensis

This long-lived armored giant reaches maturity between the ages of fifteen for males and twenty for females. But theBaikal sturgeon, has struggled to bounce back since it was dangerously overfished in the early twentieth century. Despite bans on fishing them, pollution in the shallow waters where the sturgeon spawns have halted the species' recovery.

5. Worm
Manayunkia baicalensis

This polychaete is a tube worm that lives at the bottom of the lake. It forms protective tubes around its body with sand, rock, and silt. The worm sprouts a crown of tentacles that fan out of the tubes and help the creature breathe.

Species that live in
SLOW-MOVING FRESH WATER

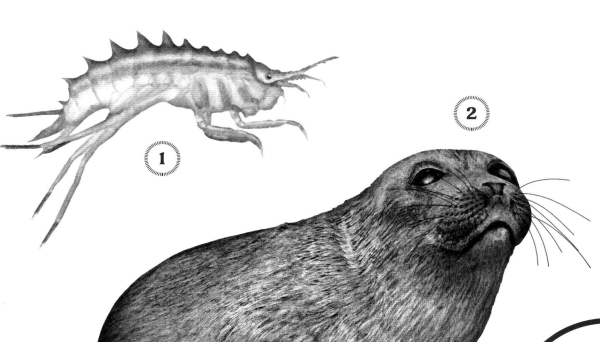

A unique ecosystem

More than 7,000 miles of mountains and tundra separate the nerpa from its closest relative, the Arctic ringed seal. But the world's lone freshwater seal endures similar threats to its cousin. This species is threatened by poaching. There are efforts to curb the killing. Russian authorities banned nerpa hunting completely, though poaching still takes place.

6. Baikal black grayling
Thymallus baicalensis

The Baikal black grayling inhabits the coasts and bays of the lake, where it feeds on insects. To catch some flying bugs, these fish—who are cousins of the salmon family—will jump roughly 1.5 feet into the air. Sensitive to poor water quality, these fish are under particular threat from climate change.

7. Baikal omul
Coregonus migratorius

As its scientific name implies, the Baikal omul swims out of the lake and into surrounding rivers to spawn each year in September and October. This fish has been migrating since prehistoric times. Scientists believe the Baikal omul traveled inland to the lake from the Arctic Ocean nearly 20,000 years ago.

8. Baikal oilfish
Comephorus baicalensis

The Baikal oilfish is specially adapted to swim in the lake's depths, which go more than 3,000 feet down. The oilfish lacks a swim bladder and grows two large pectoral fins that almost look like dragonfly wings, making it easier to travel under intense pressure. Native Siberians used the oil from this fish to light lamps, earning them their name.

9. Water silk
Spirogyra

Water silk is an invasive species of freshwater algae that started taking over shallow waters on Lake Baikal in the early 2010s. The algae favors warmer weather, and would normally die off in the colder months. But climate change and water pollution are making it easier for the algae to survive and spread.

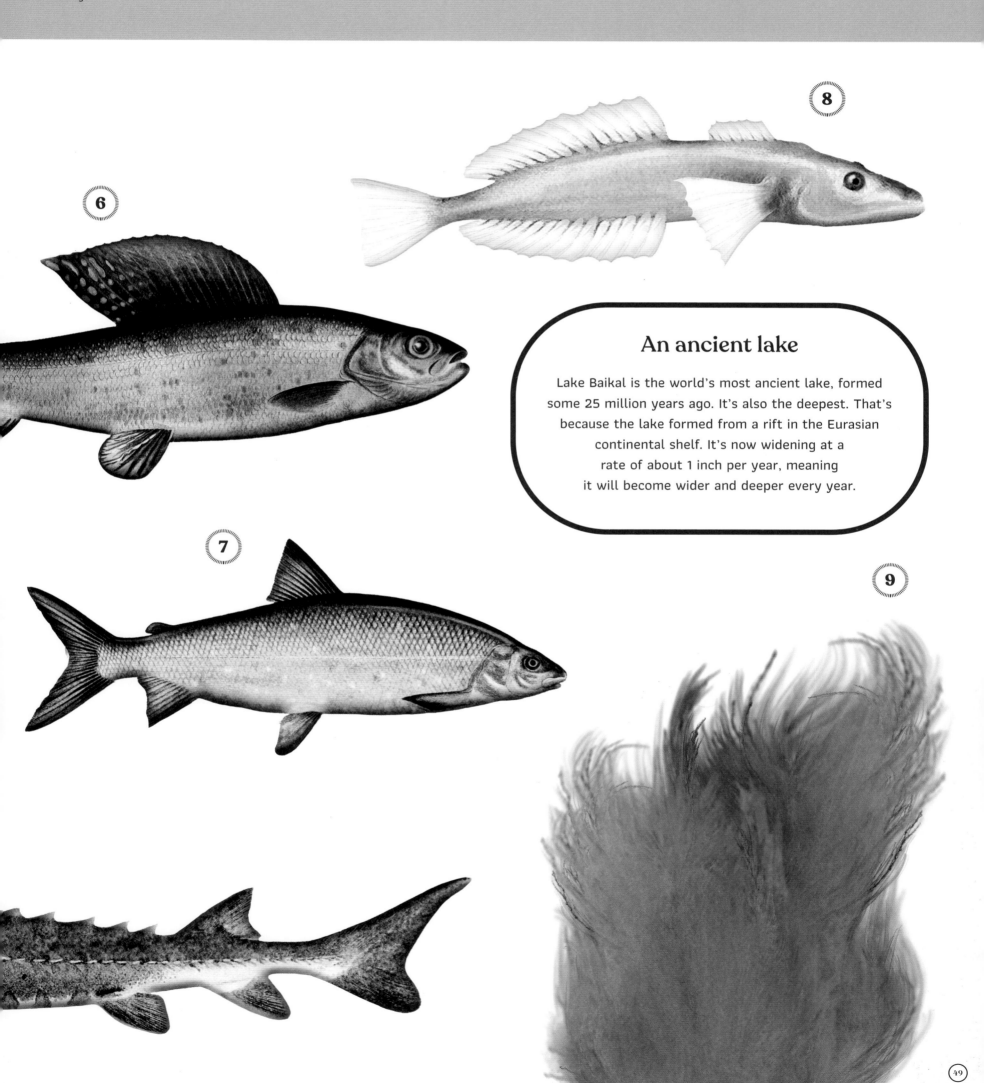

An ancient lake

Lake Baikal is the world's most ancient lake, formed some 25 million years ago. It's also the deepest. That's because the lake formed from a rift in the Eurasian continental shelf. It's now widening at a rate of about 1 inch per year, meaning it will become wider and deeper every year.

FAST-MOVING FRESH WATER

The mighty Amazon River forges a brown, snaking ribbon more than 4,000 miles across South America. The river begins in central Peru, fed by the Mantaro River, and empties into the Atlantic Ocean on Brazil's northeastern coast. It is the world's second longest river after the Nile in North Africa. The river serves as the central artery in the Amazon, the planet's biggest rainforest, home to 30 million people and one in ten animal species.

The river and its banks are dense with greenery and life. Mangrove trees weave tight root baskets and form thick walls of foliage in which colorful macaws perch. The reptiles here are prehistoric. Hefty black caimans and mata mata turtles with long necks outstretched lurk, awaiting unsuspecting prey. A green anaconda swims through the water, ready to wrap its 26 feet of constricting muscle around a deer or other large animal. The mammals, too, seem like they're from another time. Giant otters, whose families are known as romps, nestle

along the banks of the river. The plants, too, are huge. Giant water lilies provide bright green platforms big enough for a couple of kids to sit on.

The gigantism also applies to the finned denizens of this river. Pirarucu, 6-foot-long fish, swim through the rough currents like armor-plated missiles. Black, blood-sucking leeches grow to around 1.5 feet long and quietly wait for a host to latch onto. What some other creatures lack in size, they make up for in group strength or special weapons.

Red-bellied piranhas hunt in vast schools, chomping prey in fearsome mob-like feeding frenzies. Electric eels, meanwhile, produce actual zaps of electricity to stun their target.

Yet this marvelous, ancient jungle is one of the world's most threatened. Humans come here to seek their fortunes. On the river's tributaries, prospectors stir the murky bottom with giant vacuums, looking for gold, using toxic mercury which they then dump into the river. Loggers' chain saws now join the loud

din of animal calls. And ranchers, seeking more land to grow soybeans or raise cattle for beef, light destructive fires that transform vibrant jungle into ash. This is a major crisis. If humans don't preserve the Amazon, it will be almost impossible to save the world from global warming. Thankfully, Indigenous tribes who live along the Amazon River and environmentalists are teaming up to fight for new protections.

1. Green anaconda
Eunectes murinus

Eunectes murinus can grow up to 26 feet and hunt prey as big as deer. Unlike other predatory snakes in the Amazon, it has no venom to kill its food. Instead, the behemoth, olive-green snake coils its powerful, muscular body around its prey and constricts them to death, then eats its meal whole.

2. Giant leech
Haementeria ghilianii

The giant leech lives up to its name, growing up to 1.5 feet long. Unlike its European cousins, which latch onto a host and suck blood that comes to the surface of the host's skin, this creature has a long, tubular proboscis that sometimes stretches 4 inches in length and burrows into its prey to suck blood from deep in the flesh.

3. Electric eel
Electrophorus electricus

The electric eel has up to three organs that produce electricity. One organ emits weak pulses of electricity to help locate its prey. Once the eel—which, despite looking like a traditional eel, is actually a type of knifefish— finds the fish it wishes to eat, it produces a much stronger jolt of electricity, stunning its prey and allowing the hunter to strike.

4. Giant otter
Pteronura brasiliensis

The giant otter grows to more than 3 feet in length and travels in family pods of up to eight animals. This species and its kin like to make themselves at home. When they find a comfortable spot to rest, the otters tamp down plants and leaves and create little nests for themselves.

5. Mata mata
Chelus fimbriata

This freshwater turtle's distinct, triangular head blends into leaves on the river. But its shape does more than just provide cover— it extends its long neck above the surface rapidly and opens its mouth as wide as it can, creating a suction that draws prey into its powerful jaws.

Species that live in
FAST-MOVING FRESH WATER

6. Giant water lily

Victoria amazonica

There are few plants like the giant water lily, which spreads its goliath leaves on the surface of the water, sometimes reaching 10 feet across. The stalks that sprout from below the water are even longer, sometimes growing to 26 feet in length. Its flowers are so huge, it can take two days for them to open, turning from white to pink from the first night to the second.

7. Payara

Hydrolycus scomberoides

The silvery payara can grow more than 3 feet long. What stands out most about its appearance are the two enormous fangs that sprout from its bottom jaw, which it uses to impale its prey. These distinctive denticles—with which it hunts down fearsome prey such as piranhas—have led to it being known as the vampire fish.

8. Red-bellied piranha

Pygocentrus nattereri

Of all four major species of piranha, this is the fiercest. The red-bellied piranha is a notorious predator, known to hunt in schools of up to 100. Their sharp teeth and powerful jaws allow a group of these fish to tear apart birds, fish, and other prey much larger than itself. Though there's little reason for humans to fear these animals, in reality, they are unlikely to attack.

9. Black caiman

Melanosuchus niger

While the black caiman is most closely related to other caimans, these giant crocodilians look more like American alligators and can grow more than 20 feet long, making them the Amazon's largest predators. Black caimans feed mostly on fish and mollusks, though the reptiles are known to attack humans.

10. Pirarucu

Arapaima gigas

The pirarucu is a river giant, the world's largest freshwater fish, growing to 6 feet or more. In water with too little oxygen, these fish can come to the surface and breathe air. It belongs to a family of heavy tropical river fish known as the bony tongues thanks to—you guessed it—the teeth that grow on their tongues.

A unique ecosystem

Approximately 20 percent—or one fifth—of the world's fresh river water is discharged through the Amazon River network into the ocean. At more than 2.5 million square miles, it is the biggest drainage basin in the world. During the rainy season, the river rises 30 feet, flooding the surrounding land and more than tripling the area covered by water.

WETLANDS

The Norfolk Broads are an icon of the English country idyll. Streams and rivers snake between tufts of Norfolk reeds. Windmills stand watch quietly over the rippling waters. Thatched roof cottages sit on placid lakes, known as broads.

These 117 square miles of wetland on England's eastern coast have long been a place where the human and natural worlds meet. At least as far back as the 1100s, the woodlands near the Norfolk Broads were cleared. For the next two centuries, digging out the peatlands in the area served as a major industry. By the 1500s, peat digging saw a rapid decline. That was in part to natural causes and to the outbreak of the Black Plague, which killed many of the workers who once did the labor-intensive job of digging.

Water soon filled the trenches and holes, creating the 124 miles of navigable waterways that define the Broads today.

People aren't the only land creatures that like to navigate atop the Norfolk Broads' river system. Fen raft spiders stretch eight legs out to skim on the surface of the calm water, often taking shelter on the green pads of floating pennywort. Water voles, little rodents with dark brown fur and beady eyes, swim in the water but make their homes in burrows on land. Members of a rare species of swallowtail butterflies glint yellow as they flutter among the white blossoms of lesser water plantain. Western marsh harriers find the breams that swim along the rivers a tasty meal and will dive from above to snatch the fish in their sharp talons.

The greenery and foliage in the Norfolk Broads play a vital role in combating climate change. According to the British government, this wetland landscape has sucked 42 million tons of carbon dioxide, the main gas heating the planet, out of the atmosphere and stored it in its peat and soil over the past 12,000 years. That equals more carbon pollution than all the coal-burning power plants in the United Kingdom produce in a year. But this ecosystem is also at risk. This low-lying area close to the coast risks being flooded with seawater if ocean levels rise by as much as scientists predict they could by midcentury.

1. Water vole
Arvicola amphibius

The water vole is a homebody. These amphibious rodents live in small families and rarely leave a home range that they mark with scents scratched from glands on their hind feet. They nibble a tidy lawn on the doorstep of their burrow and form a pathway down to the water's edge through repeated journeys back and forth.

2. Bream
Abramis brama

The freshwater bream is one of the most common river and lake fish, and it thrives in the Broads. It can survive out of water for extended periods of time and can feed on a wide range of prey, from insects, mollusks, and plants to filter-feeding on plankton. They're also widely fed upon by humans who like to fish.

3. Floating pennywort
Hydrocotyle ranunculoides

Originally from Central and South America, floating pennywort arrived in Britain in the early 1980s as an ornamental aquatic plant. From there, it took over. These invasive plants can grow up to 8 inches per day and regenerate from a small fragment. Scientists are now examining ways to use insects or fungi to control the population.

4. Burbot
Lota lota

These marbled grey and yellow bottom dwellers, which can grow to more than 12 inches long, disappeared in the 1960s and were long believed extinct. But there's a potentially happy turn of events: In 2020, British conservation officials reintroduced this freshwater relative of the codfish in hopes a wild population may once again thrive here.

5. Norfolk reed
Phragmites australis

This common reed may seem unremarkable, but it might be the most important living being in the Norfolk Broads. The reeds' dense network of roots dig down nearly 6.5 feet and help hold riverbeds and earth in place, preserving vital habitats for other plants and animals and protecting this region against erosion.

Species that live in
WETLANDS

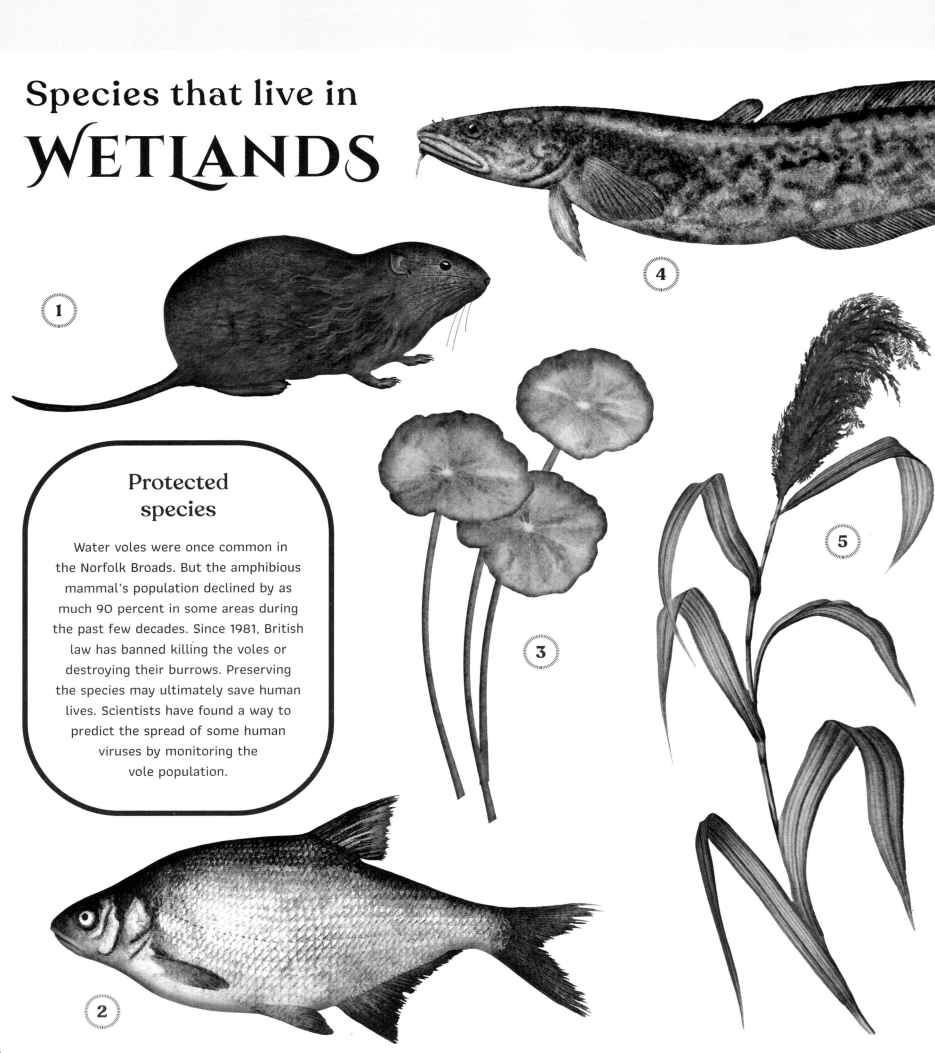

Protected species

Water voles were once common in the Norfolk Broads. But the amphibious mammal's population declined by as much 90 percent in some areas during the past few decades. Since 1981, British law has banned killing the voles or destroying their burrows. Preserving the species may ultimately save human lives. Scientists have found a way to predict the spread of some human viruses by monitoring the vole population.

6. Western marsh harrier
Circus aeruginosus

The Western marsh harrier's meter-plus wingspan allows it to soar on handsome tricolored wings—a mix of mahogany, cream and grey—over the marsh in search of fish and rodents as prey. These raptors are widespread across Europe and Africa, but habitat loss threatened the population in Britain—until the 1980s. Since then, this bird has bounced back, making it one of England's most successful conservation stories.

7. Lesser water plantain
Baldellia ranunculoides

The lesser water plantain doesn't bear the banana-like fruit found in many supermarkets. But it does produce elegant, pale-pink blossoms during the summer months. Its scientific name comes from the Latin word for *buttercup*. Though the two plants' blooms look nothing alike, they have similarly shaped seeds.

8. Swallowtail butterfly
Papilio machaon britannicus

Smaller and weaker than its continental European cousins, the British swallowtail butterfly are under threat. These dazzling insects, with black and soft-yellow wings, are found only in the Broads and are threatened by the rising sea levels consuming their homes. But research shows the British swallowtail butterfly is breeding with their hardier European relatives as they move north to cooler climates.

9. Fen raft spider
Dolomedes plantarius

The fen raft spider is one of Europe's largest and rarest spiders, and it has a rather magical skill: It uses the water like a web. It can swim underwater, but typically these eight-legged arachnids stand on the riverbank's edge, or a plant's stem, and dip two feet into the still waters to feel for vibrations from its prey.

Ancient survivors

Just west of the Norfolk Broads sits the King Oak. This ancient tree was a sapling during the Battle of Hastings, when the Normans invaded England in 1066. Today the gnarled oak is perhaps the most famous resident of the Fairhaven Woodland and Water Garden.

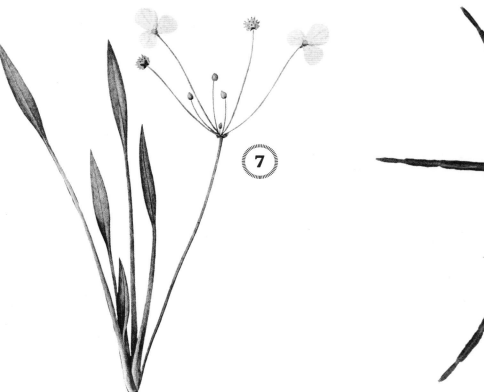

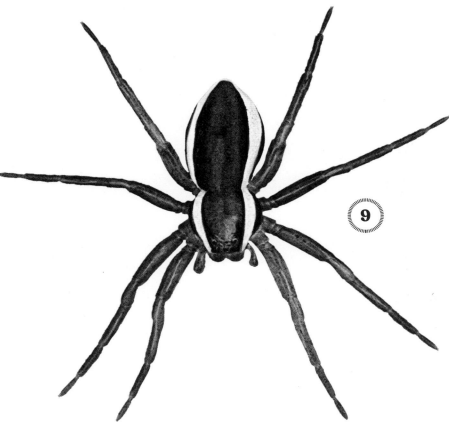

VENTS AND SEEPS

The Galápagos Rift is a giant valley deep underwater, located 250 miles northeast of the famous Ecuadorian island chain in the eastern Pacific that bears the same name.

The rift is formed in the location where two tectonic plates—the Cocos to the north and the Nazca to the south—diverge and spread apart. The enormous canyon forms ridges close to 2 miles wide.

There is virtually no light at depths of around 8,200 feet. For decades, scientists believed life could not survive that deep. But in 1977, scientists detected dramatic temperature spikes of up to 752° Fahrenheit, which is almost four times the boiling point of water. Using special robotic submersibles, the researchers ultimately discovered hydrothermal

vents—sort of like deep-sea geysers or hot springs. So why doesn't it boil? Pressure. Diving down 33 feet doubles the pressure you would feel from the ordinary atmosphere on land. A hydrothermal vent at 8,200 feet feels like 250 atmospheres—pressure which would crush a human. But some creatures thrive in the superhot underwater vents, which spew chemicals and minerals like chimneys. These take the place of sunlight to feed plants that form the bottom rung of the food ladder. Bacteria form expansive mats millimeters thick with microorganisms. The bacteria in turn provide food for giant red-tipped tube worms that grow like fields of hard, crusted tulips along the base of the chimney vents. Giant white clams—whose soft bodies are prized as a delicacy by small vent crabs—capture nitrogen that gurgles from the vents.

The more scientists study this remote area, the more remarkable discoveries are made. In 2018, researchers discovered that deep-sea skates, a stingray-like relative of sharks, actually incubate their eggs near the warmth of the vents. Hydrothermal vents also help scientists better understand what life on other planets might be like. The intensity of this environment suggests life could exist in extreme circumstances on other planets. That's right—the deep-sea rift helps us better model the possibility of aliens.

1. Vent fish
Thermarces cerberus

The vent fish looks a bit like a greyish-pink blade swimming through the darkness of the vents. They are important predators. This fish will feast on limpets, clearing them off the tube worms and making room for new baby tube worms to grow.

2. Giant white clam
Calyptogena magnifica

The giant white clam lives up to 25 years in these quiet, dark depths alongside the vents. Like many other clams, this bivalve is a suspension feeder, meaning it captures nitrogen and fatty compounds—spewed from the vents and suspended in the water—to satisfy its hunger. Little more is known about this species, since it is so challenging to observe in the wild.

3. White crab
Bythograea thermydron

This is one of the deepest-dwelling crabs in the world. These tiny crustaceans' eyes are adapted to pick up the dimmest bits of light emitted by the vents themselves. They also feed on bacteria that produce carotenoids, a type of organic pigment found in carrots and tomatoes, which gives the eggs the female crabs lay a red color.

4. Red-tipped tube worm
Riftia pachyptila

Red-tipped tube worms have no jaws or guts. Instead, these giant, deepwater creatures' bodies—which can grow more than 10 feet tall—have a special organ called a trophosome, where it stores bacteria that use chemicals to manufacture the worm's food.

Species that live in VENTS AND SEEPS

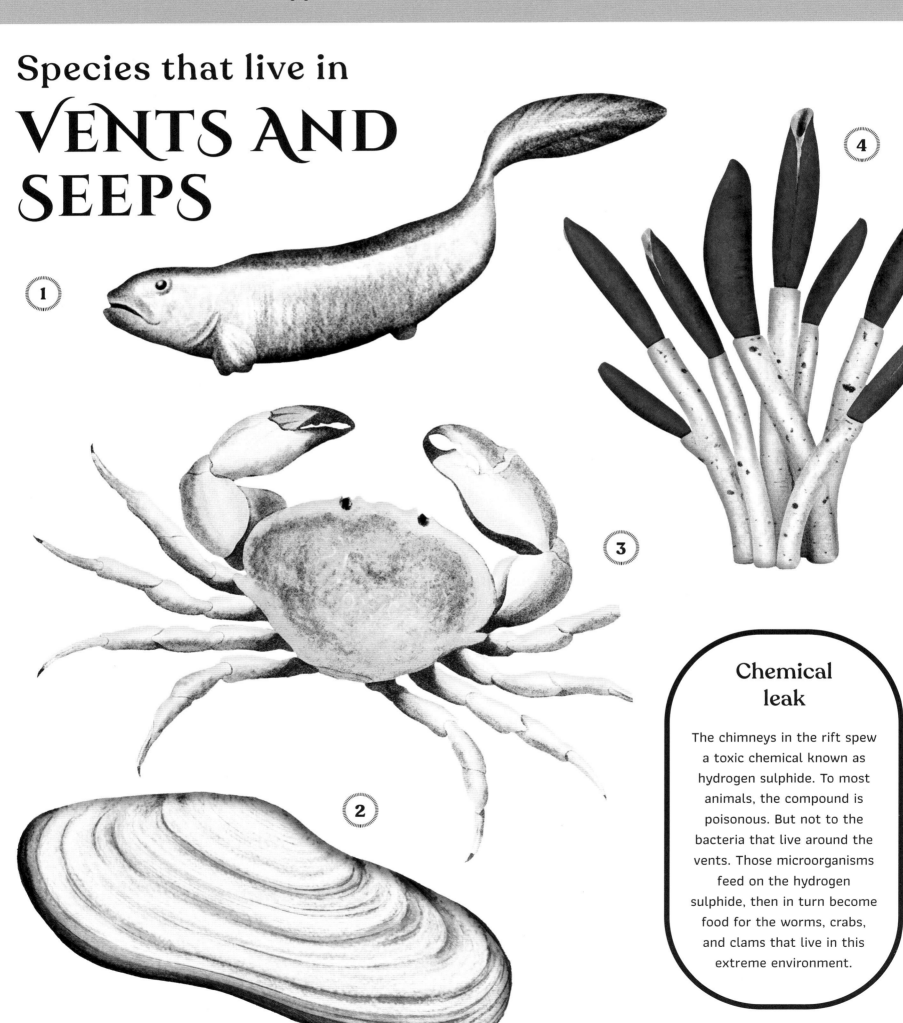

Chemical leak

The chimneys in the rift spew a toxic chemical known as hydrogen sulphide. To most animals, the compound is poisonous. But not to the bacteria that live around the vents. Those microorganisms feed on the hydrogen sulphide, then in turn become food for the worms, crabs, and clams that live in this extreme environment.

5. Purple sea cucumber
Pelagothuria natatrix

These dazzling creatures, which look somewhat like a jellyfish, will sometimes appear close to the seafloor, but swim up and down the water column. That makes the purple sea cucumber what scientists call truly pelagic, though it only rarely drifts this deep down.

6. Feather-duster worm
Sabellastarte spectabilis

The feather-duster worm produces a fluffy tuft that looks like ostrich feathers. But these aren't decorative. This creature is covered in bacteria that help it turn methane seeping from the vents into energy. It needs no mate to reproduce and can simply fragment to create a second being.

7. Bacterial mats
Beggiatoa

These microscopic organisms cluster around vents in sprawling mats up to 0.5 millimeters thick. Like many creatures in this lightless depth, it can appear white. That's because the bacteria store sulphur in their cells.

8. Limpet
Neomphalus fretterae

These tiny sea snails look almost like barnacles at the bottom of the sea. Like barnacles, they also cling to a host. For these limpets, that host is the long, white stems of red-tipped tube worms.

9. Deep-sea octopus
Graneledone boreopacifica

Like most octopuses, the deep-sea variety dies after reproducing just once. But what makes this octopus so unique is that it broods its eggs over 53 months. It's thought the cold temperatures could explain this brooding period—longer than any other animal known to scientists at more than four years!

Diversity in the depths

The discovery of the Galápagos Rift hydrothermal vents in 1977 revolutionized the scientific understanding of where and how life could exist on Earth. The temperature, depth, darkness, and presence of toxic chemicals make this ecosystem uninhabitable for many species, but researchers were amazed to find the diversity of life that exists around the vents. In the decades since, hundreds of other deep-sea hydrothermal vents have been discovered.

DEEP WATER

The Tyrrhenian Sea covers a more than 106,200-square-mile basin stretching west from Italy to the islands of Corsica and Sardinia. On average, the seafloor is 6,526 feet deep.

This sea has occupied the human imagination for millennia. Named for the Etruscans, the civilization that occupied Italy before the rise of the Romans, the sea served for centuries as a major trading hub for peoples from across Europe, Africa, and Asia. Today it functions similarly, drawing fishermen, tourists, and traders from around the world.

In much the same way that this sea is a meeting point for different peoples, it also marks where the Adriatic and Ionian tectonic plates meet and force one another back toward the Earth's center. This causes the formation of underwater volcanoes such as Marsili, a behemoth some 109 miles south of Naples that

rises close to 1,500 feet off the seafloor. The nature under the waves is similarly varied. Particularly in the south of the sea, corals abound. There are zigzag corals, branching out like surreal desert shrubs, and Mediterranean black corals, which, despite their name, appear white. The corals live among other slow-moving creatures, too. Lollipop sponges sprout like beige

candy from the sandy bottom. Slate pen sea urchins, their spines encompassing most of their bodies, crawl along the bottom like nearly 4-inch underwater naval mines.

The finfish that define the cuisine of this region are abundant. Silver pomfrets and imperial blackfish swim in schools, while barracudina cruise the water columns as solitary hunters.

Across the Mediterranean region, climate change is taking a heavy toll. The vast sea, of which the Tyrrhenian is a part, is

warming roughly 20 percent faster than the rest of the world. That makes it more difficult for fish and corals to survive and throws the entire ecosystem into disarray. Fishers are finding ways to survive, farming fish and instilling new rules to conserve struggling populations. But this is another region of the world that threatens to experience severe changes if humans don't rapidly scale back planet-heating pollution in the years to come.

1. Imperial blackfish

Schedophilus ovalis

The imperial blackfish is favored among fishers in the Mediterranean for its sweet, white flesh. As babies, imperial blackfish know just where to hide. The grey-colored juveniles dwell among the long, stinging tentacles of the Portuguese man-of-war for safety.

2. Plume worm

Serpula vermicularis

If you saw a plume worm from below, you might assume it was an old, white pipe covered in algae. But out of the calcite-and-aragonite-based tube it forms to protect itself blooms an orange-pink head-like structure that secretes an antibiotic mucus to protect the worm.

3. Barracudina

Sudis hyalina

The barracudina grows nearly 24 inches long and looks like an agile, toothy blade. Its rows of sharp, serrated teeth are used to feed on other fish, but that's not all they will bite. Its bite marks are sometimes found in underwater mooring cables.

4. Atlantic pomfret

Brama brama

There are nearly three dozen species of pomfret in the world, but the Atlantic variety is a silvery fish with a blunt head and long pectoral fins. These fish, which are sometimes eaten by humans, feed on smaller fish and crustaceans that cluster near corals.

Species that live in
DEEP WATER

A unique ecosystem

Due to its depth of 12,417 feet, the Tyrrhenian Sea is one of the most biodiverse parts of the Mediterranean. Its southern shoals contain massive colonies of rare deep-sea corals. The gulf off the Italian megacity of Naples is home to a vast array of bivalves, corals, and fish.

5. Splendid alfonsino

Beryx splendens

The splendid alfonsino is easy to spot with its pinkish-orange coloring. Its large yellow eyes reflect light back into its retina to help the fish see in the darkness of the deep sea, where they pass their days. At night, when it is safer from predators, they venture closer to the surface of the water.

6. Lollipop sponge

Stylocordyla pellita

It's not hard to guess how the lollipop sponge came to earn its name—it develops a bulbous "head" atop a thin stem, looking just like a childhood sweet. But that's not its whole body. *Stylocordyla pellita* grows a branching, rootlike structure that anchors it to soft sediment in the deep water.

7. Zigzag coral

Madrepora oculata

The zigzag coral provides shelter for crustaceans and fish amid its meandering white skeleton. But it makes sure to protect itself, too. This coral produces a mucus that coats itself and prevents parasites from boring into its skeleton.

8. Long-spine slate pen sea urchin

Cidaris cidaris

Cidaris cidaris—sometimes known as a long-spine slate pen sea urchin or, more simply, a pencil urchin—grows long, tubelike spikes that help it cling to the bottom. These urchins feed on algae and small invertebrates, and will sometimes devour coral.

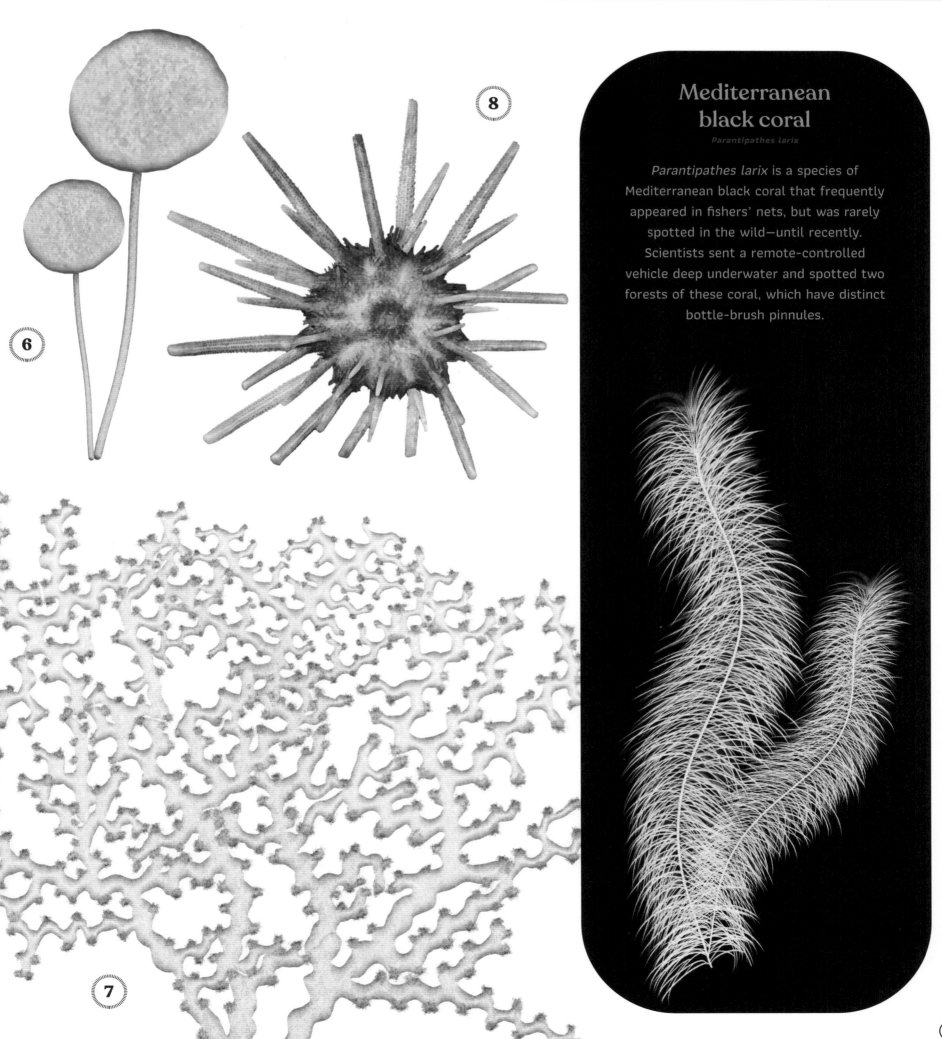

Mediterranean black coral

Parantipathes larix

Parantipathes larix is a species of Mediterranean black coral that frequently appeared in fishers' nets, but was rarely spotted in the wild—until recently. Scientists sent a remote-controlled vehicle deep underwater and spotted two forests of these coral, which have distinct bottle-brush pinnules.

INDEX

SOURCES

Animal Diversity Web

Animal Diversity Web (ADW) is an online database of animal natural history, distribution, classification, and conservation biology at the University of Michigan.

animaldiversity.org

National Geographic

The National Geographic Society (NGS) uses the power of science, exploration, education, and storytelling to illuminate and protect the wonder of our world.

nationalgeographic.com

Ocean Conservancy

A Washington, D.C.–based nonprofit that advocates for oceans across the globe. With a focus on science-based solutions, the focus is on formulating policies to save our oceans.

oceanconservancy.org

ABOUT THE CREATORS

Alexander Kaufman

Alexander is an award-winning senior reporter at HuffPost, where he writes about climate change, energy, and the environment. He's filed stories from Vietnam, Greenland, and the Brazilian Amazon. A fifth-generation New Yorker, he lives in Queens with his partner Amanda and a cat named Ashitaka.

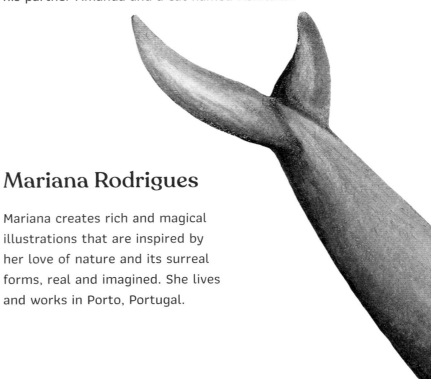

Mariana Rodrigues

Mariana creates rich and magical illustrations that are inspired by her love of nature and its surreal forms, real and imagined. She lives and works in Porto, Portugal.

The illustrations in this book were created digitally.
Set in Athiti, Milk Drops, and Recoleta.

Library of Congress Control Number 2020951411
ISBN 978-1-4197-5289-6

Text © 2021 Alexander Kaufman
Illustrations © 2021 Mariana Rodrigues
Book design by Nicola Price
Cover © 2021 Magic Cat

Printed and bound in China
10 9 8 7 6 5 4 3 2 1

Abrams Books are available at special discounts when purchased in quantity for premiums and promotions
as well as fundraising or educational use. Special editions can also be created to specification. For details, contact
specialsales@abramsbooks.com or the address below.

MIX
Paper from
responsible sources
FSC® C017606

ABRAMS The Art of Books
195 Broadway, New York, NY 10007
abramsbooks.com

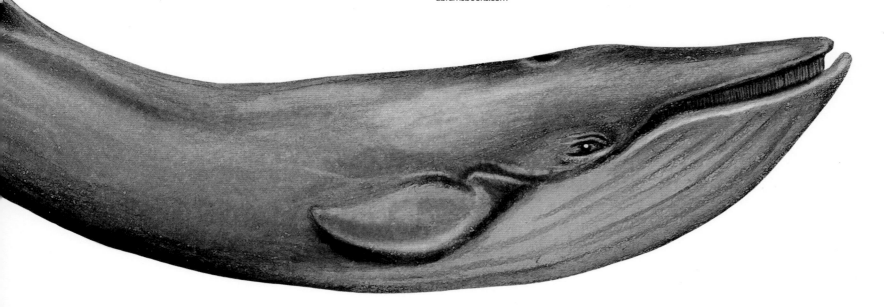